EQUALITY IN AMERICA

EQUALITY
IN AMERICA

Religion, Race, and the Urban Majority

ALAN P. GRIMES

NEW YORK
OXFORD UNIVERSITY PRESS 1964

For
Margaret, Alan, Katherine, and Peter

CONTENTS

INTRODUCTION vii

1 RELIGION 3

2 RACE 41

3 THE URBAN MAJORITY 89

INDEX 131

41974

INTRODUCTION

In a narrow sense this book is composed of three essays on topics of current interest to most Americans: religion and politics, racial segregation, and state legislative apportionment. In this narrow sense, the book is guided by three notable Supreme Court cases, the prayer in the public schools case of *Engel* v. *Vitale* (1962), the school desegregation case of *Brown* v. *Board of Education* (1954), and the legislative reapportionment case of *Baker* v. *Carr* (1962). But this book is really concerned with a much larger topic: equality in religion, race, and representation.

Equality, like freedom, involves a relationship. If every man seeks to be free, every freedom-seeking man becomes in some way an obstacle in the path of someone else's freedom. For questions of freedom eventually resolve themselves into questions of "whose freedom to do what, affecting whom?" Historically, the question of "whose freedom?" has tended to be answered by the query "whose power?" Thus, were absolute freedom possible, it would have consisted of nothing less than absolute power. Yet, as political power became ever more broadly based, its correlative, freedom, became more widely distributed. A decision on matters of religious faith, for instance, once the prerogative of the king, later the privilege of Parliament, became eventually the choice of individuals, as the base of public power changed. The democratization of power, however, introduced a new problem in the determination of freedom. As much of the history of the eighteenth and nineteenth centuries demonstrated, democracy in America led to an unequal division of freedom, granting superior freedom to the majority who were Protestant in religion and white in race. In time, such an unequal distribution of freedom was challenged.

Because of the difficulty of arriving at a satisfactory standard for discriminating between people whose claimed freedoms were in conflict, the measure of equality has taken on ever-increasing significance as a legitimate solution to the problem. Equality has thus provided a standard for settling disputes over freedom which, if left to the self-interests of the disputants alone, could seldom be amicably settled, for such questions as whose church and whose race are hardly matters upon which men will agree, if indeed they are properly put political questions at all. Where there is no accepted standard of proof, it is fruitless to dispute claimed superiorities. Equality, as an ethical standard, recognizes the diversity of men and acknowledges differentiation while rejecting invidious discrimination; it does not, its proponents argue, level men to the lowest common denominator, but elevates them to the highest common dignity. The principle of equality, considered in this light, does not declare that all men are in fact equal; it does declare that allegations of religious and racial superiority cannot be proven, and, therefore, in the interest of public peace men ought to treat each other in these affairs as though they were equal.

The development of this principle for settling conflicts has been centuries in the making and has been brought about more by necessity than by desire. Men have associated attitudes of superiority with their own situations whenever they have had the power to enforce their views. Puritans were reluctant to grant equality to Quakers; Protestants were reluctant to grant equality to Catholics; Christians were reluctant to grant equality to Jews; whites have been reluctant to grant equality to Negroes. Immigration, however, produced religious and racial diversity in America, and democracy armed each new generation with the power to contest the claimed superiorities of previous settlers.

In general, the path to equality has led through the large urban centers, where diversity of religion and race has been historically brought about by immigration and migration. For generations of immigrants the urban centers have provided not only a gateway into American life but have in turn shaped the conditions and the values of that life. When immigration was restricted, following the First World War, American Negroes commenced that extraordinary migration into the cities which has in turn so vitally affected the politics and values of America at large. Native American Negroes are following the pathway to equality marked out by generations of immigrants. The majority of Negroes today are members of an urban majority in America. "Freedom now" has taken on significance because the majority of Negroes live in urban areas and have therefore the power which is the political prerequisite for freedom. The close proximity of diverse people in cities has necessitated the norm of religious and racial equality in these areas in the interest of domestic peace; the emergence of African and Asian nationalism soon after the racism of the Axis powers in World War II has contributed to the acceptance of equality as a necessity of international peace.

In urban America the whole complex of problems related to religious and racial minorities has coalesced into one large issue. No branch of the government is immune from this conflict over values and public policy; both political parties are divided over the issue. It may be said that there exist two constituencies behind American politics—one, essentially cosmopolitan and urban-oriented, which seeks to push forward the policy of equality; the other, essentially provincial and rural-oriented, seeks to maintain in religion, race, and politics its superiorities of the past. White, Protestant, rural America pulls in one direction; urban America, with its diversity of religions and races, pulls in the other. The differing compositions of the constituencies give rise to different values.

The urban majority is proving to be a liberating force in American politics, redistributing freedom by equalizing the claims of the contestants. Equality is proving, practically, to be a standard which satisfies at once the requirements of power and of legitimacy. It is a second-best solution in which none has perfect freedom; the first-choice claims of some for superiority are put aside in order to avoid the subjugation which would be the worst solution for others.

American politics has always made a pragmatic adjustment to its immediate needs, tempering its idealism with expediency. Today, ironically, the imperatives of urban life are making expedient the fulfillment of the historic ideal of equality.

I have incurred many obligations in preparing this book. I am particularly indebted to Samuel Krislov and Joseph Schlesinger of Michigan State University and S. Sidney Ulmer of the University of Kentucky for reading portions of the manuscript, and to Russel B. Nye of Michigan State University for reading the entire manuscript. All were most helpful in their suggestions, comments, and criticisms; none, of course, are responsible in any way for the conclusions I arrived at. I am also indebted to the All-University Research Committee of Michigan State University for making funds available to assist with the costs of research and manuscript preparation.

I RELIGION

THE QUIET fact which emerged from the discussion of religion in politics in the 1960 Presidential election was not that one candidate was a Catholic, but rather that his opponent was a Quaker. Two hundred years ago, on the eve of the American Revolution, it would have been inconceivable that either a Catholic or a Quaker could ever aspire to high public office and even less credible that he should have great popular support in doing so. Three hundred years ago in much of colonial America both Catholics and Quakers were looked upon as subversives. By a coincidence, the last time a Quaker candidate ran for the Presidency, in 1928, he also ran against a Catholic. The fact that in both of these contests between Catholic and Quaker candidates the religious focus was on the Catholic rather than the Quaker aspirant reveals in part the extent to which the once ostracized and often banished Quakers have become accepted in American life; and the election of a Catholic in 1960 gives promise that the time is not too distant when the religious convictions of candidates for public office, be they Protestant, Catholic, Jew, or atheist, will no longer be matters of public concern, for the fundamental course of American politics has marked the increasing realization, both in law and practice, of the equality of men in their religious freedom.

The rise of religious freedom has been in large measure the unintended result of our early history, prompted by accident, conditioned by necessity. It has been at once the triumph of our experience over our initial ideology, and the triumph of diversity over uniformity. It has marked the settling for the second-best alternative—religious equality—where no religion was able to achieve that perfect freedom which comes with perfect power.

The early Protestant religions, like the Catholic, could provide no answer to the vexing question how a community, divided in its religious allegiance, could live in peace, for Protestants generally assumed that there could be only one true faith. To suggest that such a fundamental belief as religion could be made a matter of the free choice of worshipers would have appeared as ridiculous as to suggest that students should have free choice in the methods and conclusions of a problem in arithmetic. The typical position of the early Protestants was that they were not offering any innovations in religion; they were simply reforming or purifying the church, as they saw it, in accordance with Biblical teaching. As the concept of a single Christian religion and a single Christian church was preserved by Protestants, the issue of freedom to choose an alternative doctrine or church could not properly arise.

Furthermore, in accordance with the belief in royal absolutism, sanctified by the divine right theory of kings, rulers in much of Europe had the unquestioned right to establish the official creed for society. By the middle of the sixteenth century some German principalities were Lutheran, others Catholic, France was Catholic, Geneva was Calvinist, and the English under Elizabeth had formed their own national church on the Thirty-Nine Articles of Faith. The issue of religious freedom could not arise as long as there was believed to be only one church, one doctrine, one pathway to salvation, and that the one legally sanctioned by secular authority. Calvin's *Institutes of the Christian Religion* (1536), which became Holy Word to many of the early settlers of America, considered it the duty of the government "to cherish and support the external worship of God, to preserve the pure doctrine of religion, to defend the constitution of the church." [1] This recondite task was willingly undertaken by energetic governments throughout western Christendom, even though they might differ with other governments over doctrines of religion.

Three antecedent conditions, in addition to the obvious factor of diversity of belief, appear to have been most significant for the modern doctrine of religious freedom. First, the millennial dispute between the secular and spiritual branches of government for prime authority in the society had to be resolved in favor of the former. Second, nationalism had to develop to such an extent that national loyalties could be safely assumed to be superior to all other loyalties. Third, the papacy had to decline as a truly effective political power. It took centuries for these conditions to develop.

The triumph of the secular arm of government was achieved in England by the assumption of royal authority over both church and state. Needless to say, the combining of spiritual and secular authority in one ruler considerably fostered, even as it reflected, the spirit of nationalism. The rise of nationalism throughout the Continent greatly diminished the secular role of the papacy. The confusion of loyalties between church and state, between things spiritual and things political, which seems so foreign to the modern reader, was in fact a well-founded confusion in the sixteenth and seventeenth centuries. The problem of religious freedom then resembled the problem of religious freedom for Moslems in Israel today. As long as religion bore the stamp of national sanction it was bound to lead to the issue of national allegiance as well as to the locus of political power within the state. Political and religious loyalty were thus inextricably intertwined.

This conjunction of religious and political allegiance was seen in the terrible War of Religion in France, late in the sixteenth century. It was not only a war of the Huguenots and Catholics, but a crucial political conflict over the succession to the throne in France in which the Huguenots appealed to Protestant rulers in Germany and England for support. The Massacre of St. Bartholomew (1572), in which the Catholics slaughtered Protestants, had far-reaching consequences. Protestant doctrine, as articulated in that classic work, *A Defense of Liberty Against Tyrants* (1579), justified foreign intervention in France on the grounds that "all histories testify that there have been neighboring princes to oppose tyranny, and maintain the people in their right. The princes of these times by imitating so worthy examples, should suppress the tyrants both of bodies and souls, and restrain the oppressors both of the commonwealth, and of the church of Christ: otherwise, they themselves, may most deservedly be branded with the infamous title of tyrant." [2] Such a doctrine could hardly sit well with French nationalists, or indeed nationalists of any country; it is little wonder that in 1620 in the reign of the Protestant James I, Cambridge University saw fit publicly to burn the book.

That the papacy was then a major temporal power was avowed by Protestant and Catholic alike. The influential Jesuit, Cardinal Bellarmine, observed in 1610 "that the Pope has the highest indirect temporal power. . . . We assert that, although the Pontiff as Pontiff does not have absolute temporal power, nonetheless for the attainment of spiritual good, he has the highest power of disposing temporal matters for the whole of Christendom." [3] Religious loyalties seemed inextricably involved in political questions of the most consequential proportions.

This mixture of politics and religion, of nationalism and theology, and the anxieties attendant on their uncertain relationship, is clearly seen in the dedicatory preface of the translators of the King James version of the Bible (1611). Great were the blessings, it was noted, which were brought to the English people when James I was sent to rule over them.

For whereas it was the expectation of many, who wished not well unto our *Sion*, that upon the setting of that bright *Occidental Star*, Queen *Elizabeth* of most happy memory, some thick and palapable clouds of darkness would so have overshadowed this Land, that men should have been in doubt which way they were to walk; and that it should hardly be known, who was to direct the unsettled State; the appearance of Your Majesty, as of the *Sun* in his strength, instantly dispelled those supposed and surmised mists, and gave unto all that were well affected exceeding cause of comfort; especially when we beheld the Government established in Your Highness, and your hopeful Seed, by an undoubted Title, and this also accompanied with peace and tranquility at home and abroad.

But among all our joys, there was no one that more filled our hearts, than the blessed continuance of the preaching of God's sacred word among us; which is that inestimable treasure, which excelleth all the riches of the earth; because the fruit thereof extendeth itself, not only to the time spent in this transitory world, but directeth and disposeth men unto that eternal happiness which is above in heaven.

The problem of religious dissent, not yet called religious freedom, lest it give the matter a favorable connotation, continued to arise, with increasing strength throughout the seventeenth century. In England loyalty oaths were established for students in an effort to ensure religious conformity. For example, Roger Williams, a student at Pembroke, an Anglican institution, was required to sign the *Subscription Book* in 1627 as a condition for receiving the A.B. degree. His signature affirmed that he would abide by the Thirty-Nine Articles of Faith decreed in 1562, that he would use the Book of Common Prayer in his worship and "no other." Futhermore, the oath affirmed: "That the King's Majesty under God is the only supreme Governour of this Realm, and of all other his Highnesse's Dominions and countries, as well in Spiritual or Ecclesiastical things or courses as temporal, and that no Foreign Prince, Person, Prelate of State or Potentate hath or ought to have any Jurisdiction, Power, Superiority, Preheminence, or Authority, Ecclesiastical or Spiritual, within his Majesty's said Realms, Dominions and Countries." [4] Loyalty oaths, however, could hardly curb the growth of religious dissent, now spurred by the increasing availability of the King James version of the Bible. It was evident that the Elizabethan settlement promulgated in the Acts of Uniformity and Supremacy of 1559 would not sufficiently contain the rising religious revolt.

When it became impossible to stamp out heresy and dissent through prosecution and persecution, emigration of dissenters appeared as a possible expedient, for it still seemed inconceivable that one political community could maintain its cohesiveness unless it embraced only one religious community. The departure of the separatist Pilgrims to Holland and later to Plymouth could provide only a small safety valve to the basic problem of keeping secure the Anglican religious monopoly within the state. Since it was felt that an established church which tolerated no dissenters was an essential concomitant of an established government, both Roman Catholic and English Calvinists struggled for control over the vast bureaucracy of the Anglican Church, which meant in effect control over the succession to the throne. Officially, at least, both Catholic and Calvinist were included as Anglicans on the rolls of the established church; in private, however, they might practice the doctrines of their particular faith. As the Puritan John Cotton wrote later in Massachusetts, "There were some scores of Godly persons in Boston, in Lincolnshire, whereof some are there still and some are here, who can witness that we entered into a covenant with the Lord and with one-another to follow after the Lord in the purity of his worship." [5] Thus the legal fiction of religious orthodoxy was maintained, even though it was violated in actual practice.

*

Traditionally, the concept of toleration has preceded the concept of religious freedom. The claim of freedom implies (when it does not assert) the possession of a right or rights; toleration turns this right into a conditioned permission. We tolerate abuses, and often those whom we do not like. As a matter of political necessity, rather than Christian charity, some degree of religious toleration developed in England in the seventeenth century. Toleration of religious dissenters was the minimum price of peace for a community which refused to abide by the "ideal" solution of absolute religious conformity. In England toleration was not given legal sanction until the Act of Toleration of 1689, which permitted non-conformists to worship while effectively disqualifying them from holding public office. Even so, however, more than a century after the defeat of the Spanish Armada by Drake, Catholics were still singled out for special discriminations. And John Locke's famous *Letter Concerning Toleration* of 1689 carefully observed, "That Church can have no right to be tolerated by the magistrate which is constituted upon such a bottom that all those who enter into it do thereby *ipso facto* deliver themselves up to the protection and service of another prince. . . . [A prince] who has not only power to persuade the members of his Church to whatsoever he lists, either as purely religious, or in order thereunto, but can also enjoin it them on pain of eternal fire." [6] Clearly the English were still concerned over the papacy as a potential temporal power.

In Colonial America, Massachusetts Bay Colony, of all the colonies, took a most intransigent stand against general toleration. Here, Nathaniel Ward, one of its most esteemed residents wrote, "All Familists, Antinomians, Anabaptists and other Enthusiasts shall have free liberty to keep away from us." [7] With what appears to have been a ferocious tenacity the Puritans insisted upon an orthodoxy of Calvinism even though, as Roger Williams aptly pointed out, they had not separated themselves from the English Church. They were, in other words, non-conformers in the English Church, insisting on their own brand of conformity.

In the great manuscript debate between John Cotton and Roger Williams after the latter's banishment from the Bay Colony, it was evident that Cotton simply did not understand what Williams was talking about, any more than did the English censor who ordered "the publick Burning of Mr. *Williams* his Booke, intitled, etc. the Tolerating of all Sorts of Religion." [8] What Williams was maintaining became substantially the modern position in America, while Cotton held to a position which was rapidly becoming outdated even in England. To Williams there was no justification for persecution for cause of conscience; it was not commanded in the Bible, and the consequences of persecution were destructive of the peace of the community. To Cotton, on the contrary, the issue was essentially whether or not a man truly abided by the dictates of his conscience. A conscience "rightly informed" ought not to be persecuted, Cotton argued, and "for an erroneous and blind conscience, (even in fundamental and weighty points) it is not lawful to persecute any, till after admonition once or twice. . . . And then if any one persist, it is not out of conscience, but against his conscience. . . . So that if such a man, after such admonition, shall still persist in the error of his way, and be therefore punished, he is not persecuted for cause of conscience, but for sinning against his own conscience." [9] In effect, all other religious persuasions other than Mr. Cotton's were in error; if after dutiful study and reflection on the points of difference one did not embrace Cotton's truth, one sinned against his conscience and warranted punishment.

What makes the position of Williams especially significant for future America is the pragmatic quality of his argument. Essentially, Williams was concerned with the consequences of a policy of persecution in comparison with a policy of toleration. An enforced policy of religious uniformity, he wrote,

sooner or later, is the greatest occasion of civil war, ravishing of conscience, persecution of Christ Jesus in his servants, and of the hypocrisy and destruction of millions of souls. . . . An enforced uniformity of religions throughout a nation or civil state, confounds the civil and religious, denies the principles of Christianity and civility. . . . The permission of other consciences and worships than a state professeth, only can, according to God, procure a firm and lasting peace; good assurance being taken, according to the wisdom of the civil state, for uniformity of civil obedience from all sorts. . . . True civility and Christianity may both flourish in a state or kingdom, notwithstanding the permission of diverse and contrary conscience, either of Jew or Gentile.[10]

And, in answer to Cotton's distinction on the character of conscience, Williams observed, "He that kills and he that is

killed, they both cry out, 'It is for God and for their conscience.' " [11]

In Williams's pleas for religious toleration, emphasis is con-
tinuously placed on the distinct and separate character of the
political or civil from the religious community, and on the
need for continuing this distinction as a matter of public
policy in order to preserve peace in the community. Secular
peace, in effect, may be separate from spiritual accord, political loyalty ought not to be confused with religious allegiance.

Oh! how lost are the sons of men in this point! To illustrate this:
—the church, or company of worshippers, whether true or false, is
like unto a body or college of physicians in a city—like unto a corporation, society, or company of East India or Turkey merchants,
or any other society or company in London; which companies
may hold their courts, keep their records, hold disputations, and
in matters concerning their society may dissent, divide, break into
schisms and factions, sue and implead each other at the law, yea,
wholly break up and dissolve into pieces and nothing, and yet the
peace of the city not be in the least measure impaired or disturbed;
because the essence or being of the city, and so the well being and
peace thereof, is essentially distinct from those particular societies.
The city courts, city laws, city punishments distinct from theirs.
The city was before them, and stands absolute and entire when
such a corporation or society is taken down. . . .[12]

Clearly, in Williams's writing, the politicized state has triumphed over the ecclesiastical state as the preserver of peace
on earth; it was this point of allegiance to the secular state that
was given more explicit expression later in the century by
John Locke in his *Letter Concerning Toleration*, after the
tragic events of England's Civil War had proved the accuracy
of Williams's contention. In political theory, the argument for
religious toleration changed its character in the course of the
dispute, as the spread of sectarianism was acknowledged and
the issue shifted from the correctness of individual conscience
to the essentially political plane of social consequences.

❋

Religious toleration as a public policy lies approximately midway between a policy of persecution and one of socially accepted rights. It reflects an uneasy truce between assumed unequals in the interest of the larger goals of peace and prosperity. In the American colonies the economic goal of survival necessitated a continuing stream of immigrants to transform the wilderness and to produce the necessities of life. Yet the need for immigration was bound in the long run to weaken the demand for conformity, particularly when there were opposing orthodoxies in the colonies to conform to. In Virginia the English church was the established church; in Massachusetts the Calvinist Congregational churches composed the state-sanctioned orthodoxy. Even though eager for new immigrants, the colonies sought to maintain religious orthodoxy.

Every society seeks in some measure to perpetuate the conditions of its existence, and those in power have normally been reluctant to concede authority to a new generation of immigrants. Every society provides some system of penalties against subversives and disturbers of the peace. It is evident that in many instances those of "contrary consciences" were, in fact as well as in dogma, disturbers of the peace. When Roger Williams advanced a contrary dogma in religion in Massachusetts, he also challenged the validity of the titles by which the Bay Company held land. His banishment, therefore, served a secular as well as a religious purpose. Anne Hutchinson was clearly subversive of the established ecclesiastical order when she held discussions in her home critical of the sermons preached to the community. The zealous Quakers were certainly on the fringes of anarchism when they disclaimed oath-taking, the immemorial manifestation of loyalty. And, one may ask, would a community today abide with the curious form of protest in which a Quaker woman ran naked through the streets to signify her displeasure with public policy?

In other words, the issue of religious freedom was initially quite clouded with the prior issue of the peace of the accepted, established order of the community; many of those whom history has properly judged to have been martyrs to the cause of freedom were very likely contumacious characters who made extraordinary demands upon the patience of their fellow man. As long as religious orthodoxy and public power were directly associated, religious dissenters suffered the awesome consequences of repression. As religious repression was the manifestation of religious power in the state, so toleration was the policy of a state in which the distribution of power among religious groups was such that those in power could not successfully impose their orthodoxy without sustained violence. In the American colonies it was in the long run the continued immigration of diverse dissenters which effectively brought about this new distribution of power.

In Virginia the charter reflected the political power in England of the English church. The English church in Virginia was given a legal monopoly; all competition among other producing and consuming units of religious persuasion was prohibited. In 1628 Lord Baltimore, a Roman Catholic, visited Virginia. As a Catholic he could not take the oath of supremacy of the Anglican church which was required in Virginia. He was, therefore, not permitted to remain in the colony, even though there was no question of his allegiance to the established order. Subsequently, Catholics were disfranchised in Virginia, and any priests who might come there were ordered to be expelled. Puritan ministers were ordered out of Virginia. Quakers were prohibited from landing there, and shipmasters transporting them into the colony were subjected to a heavy fine. Governor Berkeley, in his zeal for orthodoxy, wrote: "But I thank God there are no free schools nor printing; and I hope we shall not have these hundred years: for learning has brought disobedience and heresy and sects into the world and printing has divulged them and libels against the best government. God keep us from both!" [13]

In Massachusetts the Congregational orthodoxy was equally firmly entrenched. The Congregational churches, like the Anglican church in Virginia, were supported by taxation, and attendance at church services was required. Indeed, the franchise was restricted to church members. Dissenters like Roger

Williams and Anne Hutchinson were banished from the colonies. Jesuits and Quakers were not only prohibited entry into the colony, but banished, if discovered. Should they return after banishment, they might suffer the death penalty. In fact this was the fate of four Quakers who insisted on returning to Massachusetts after they were banished.

Nathaniel Ward summed up the matter nicely in *The Simple Cobbler of Aggawam*, when he wrote in 1647: "God doth nowhere in His word tolerate Christian States to give tolerations to adversaries of His Truth, if they have power in their hands to prevent them." The issue of toleration as a public policy was at bottom the issue of the distribution of power among competing religious groups in the community. "My heart hath naturally detested tolerations of divers Religions or of one Religion in segregant shapes," Ward wrote. "He that unwillingly assents to it, if he examines his heart by daylight, his conscience will tell him he is either an Atheist, or an Heretick, or an Hypocrite, or at best a captive to some lust." [14] This view was similar to that expressed a generation later by President Oakes of Harvard College, when he wrote in 1673: "I look upon unbounded toleration as the first-born of all abominations." [15] "God forbid," Thomas Dudley wrote when he was Governor of Massachusetts, "that our love for the truth should be grown so cold that we should tolerate error." [16] In spite of the harsh repressive measures against religious dissenters, nonconformity continued to grow, augmented by immigration in Massachusetts and Virginia, as elsewhere in the colonies. It became increasingly evident that no one religious group in any of the colonies possessed the political power to impose its views on the rest of the community.

*

The association of a public policy of toleration with a political stalemate between religious groups may be further seen when it is observed that, generally, religious toleration has been the consequence of unsuccessful intolerance. All religious groups ostensibly seek religious freedom to practice their beliefs in a congenial climate of opinion. Ideally, perfect religious freedom for any religious group would consist in complete agreement of the total community with the religious practices of that group. However, given the presence of dissenters, of in fact competing religious groups in most realistic situations, the problem becomes one of reconciling competing freedoms under the rubric of law. Generally the claim for religious freedom has arisen only when the power to control the community's belief system has been absent or insecurely held. Therefore, it may be said that the reason for some religious groups to countenance persecution and intolerance while others counseled forbearance and laissez faire toward their adversaries should not be traced to differences of doctrine but to the strength of these groups in the religious power structure of society at the time the issue arose. Traditionally, minority religions have been the most ardent champions of religious freedoms and majority religions have only reluctantly and of necessity granted these freedoms. It is interesting to compare the policies in America of the Catholic Lord Baltimore and the Quaker William Penn with the public policies of Anglican Virginia and Puritan Massachusetts described above.

Cecil Calvert, second Lord Baltimore, was granted a charter by Charles I in 1632 for the colony of Maryland. His instructions of 1633 to the governor and commissioners of Maryland show a most remarkable point of view, in that he required of them not only that they preserve the peace and unity of the passengers en route to the new colony, but that they "suffer no scandall nor offence to be given to any of the Protestants, whereby any just complaint may hereafter be made, by them, in Virginia or in England, and that for that end, they cause all Acts of Roman Catholique Religion to be done as privately as may be, and that they instruct all the Roman Catholiques to be silent upon all occasions of discourse concerning matters of Religion; and that the said Governor and Commissioners treate the Protestants with as much mildness and favor as Justice will permitt—and this to be observed at Land as well as at Sea." [17] These instructions were followed some three years later by an oath which Lord Baltimore required of the governors of Maryland:

I will not myself or any other, directly or indirectly, trouble, molest, or discountenance any person professing to believe in Jesus Christ, for or in respect to religion: I will make no difference of persons in conferring offices, favors, or rewards, for or in respect of religion: but merely as they shall be found faithful and well deserving, and endued with moral virtues and abilities: my aim shall be public unity, and if any person or officer shall molest any person professing to believe in Jesus Christ, on account of his religion, I will protect the person molested and punish the offender.[18]

Under this generous policy toward Christians, Protestants soon outnumbered Catholics in Maryland. In 1649 the Maryland Assembly passed an act, presumably drafted by Lord Baltimore, which came to be called the Act of Toleration. It was a curious piece of legislation demanding some kinds of toleration while prohibiting others. It required belief in Jesus Christ as the son of God, and in the Holy Trinity, and it prohibited blasphemy—all under penalty of death. Yet it reaffirmed the provisions of the Governor's Oath which guaranteed that no person should be molested for religious reasons, provided that he professed to believe in Jesus Christ. Fines and imprisonment were imposed for profaning the Lord's Day, but they were also imposed for calling someone "an heritick, Scismatik, Idolator, puritan, Independent, Presbiterian, Popish Priest, Jesuite, Jesuited papist, Lutheran, Calvinist, Anabaptist, Brownish, Antinomian, Barrowist, Round head, Separatist, or any other name or terme in a reproachful manner relating to matters of Religion. . . ." [19]

Unhappily for the cause of religious liberty in Maryland, when the Puritans came to power in England the Toleration Act of 1649 was replaced by one that promised freedom of worship for Protestants and denied it to Roman Catholics. However, in 1658 Lord Baltimore received Maryland back from the Puritans and the Act of Toleration was again put into effect. But a decade later, when the Anglicans came back to power in England, the Church of England was made the established church in Maryland, and Catholics there were prohibited from public worship from then until the American Revolution.

A somewhat similar history can be recorded for Pennsylvania, where initially liberal charter provisions were restrictively modified by the course of English politics. Like the Catholics, the Quakers were much persecuted and discriminated against in England. Indeed, one of the charges against the Quakers was that their refusal to subscribe to the oath of supremacy made them "papists in disguise." It was not surprising, therefore, that William Penn sought in his charter a wide latitude for religious expression. In 1670 he had written *The Great Case of Liberty of Conscience . . . Briefly Debated and Defended,* and his pamphleteering soon led him to imprisonment in the Tower. In founding his colony, he had noted: "We must give the liberty we ask. We cannot be false to our principles. We would have none to suffer for dissent on any hand." [20] The charter of 1682 provided that the right to hold office and to elect office holders would be open to those twenty-one years of age who were of good repute and who possessed "faith in Jesus Christ." It was in all a most liberal charter for Protestants and Catholics alike. In 1682 the colonial assembly enacted a provision which was even more liberal than the Maryland Toleration Act of 1649 in that it declared:

That no person, now or at any time hereafter, Living in this Province, who shall confess and acknowledge one Almighty God to be the Creator, Upholder and Ruler of the world; And who shall profess him, or herself, Obliged in Conscience to Live peaceably and quietly under the civil government, shall in any case be molested or prejudiced for his, or her, conscientious persuasion or practice. Nor shall hee or shee at any time be compelled to frequent or maintain anie religious worship, place, or Ministry whatever, contrary to his or her mind; but shall freely and fully enjoy, his or her, Christian liberty in that respect, without any Interruption or reflection. And if any person shall deride or abuse any other for his or her different persuasion or practice in matters of religion, such person, shall be lookt upon as a Disturber of the peace and be punished accordingly.[21]

Under this law Catholics as well as Protestants might worship publicly, vote, and hold public office. However, once again politics in England forced an amendment of this liberal policy, for the government of William and Mary insisted that the discriminatory oath incorporated in the Toleration Act of 1689 be applied in Pennsylvania, thus excluding Catholics from public office. In 1705 the Pennsylvania legislature enacted these religious tests in law, in which form they remained until the American Revolution. However, it has been reported that "on the eve of the Revolution Pennsylvania was the only one of the thirteen colonies in which the services of the Roman communion were publicly held." [22] The liberality of Pennsylvania's policy is reflected in the record of the growth and strength of religious groups in that colony by the time of the Revolution. In Pennsylvania could be found the major religions from England and Germany and many minor sects as well. Thus, "of 403 different congregations, 106 were German Reformed; 68 were Presbyterian; 63 Lutherans; 61 Quakers; 33 Episcopalian; 27 Baptist; 14 Moravian; 13 Mennonites; 13 Dunker or German Baptist Brethren; 9 Roman Catholic; and 1 Dutch Reformed." Also included in the population were Schwenkfelders, Palatines, and the conservative Amish.[23]

❋

The concept of equality in religious freedom could not be logically advanced without its correlative doctrine, the separation of church and state. It is to the credit of Roger Williams that he was the first American to see this relationship and to formulate it into a guiding principle of public policy. "Having bought truth dear," he wrote, "we must not sell it cheap, not the least grain of it for the whole world; no, not for the saving of souls, though our own most precious." [24] The truth, as Williams saw it, was that only when free rein was given to diverse religious consciences, with both church and state at-

tending to their quite separate affairs, could civil peace be preserved. "Civil peace," he wrote, "what is it but *pax civitatis*, the
peace of the city, whether an English city, Scotch, or Irish
city, or further abroad, French, Spanish, Turkish city, etc. . . .
the peace of the city or kingdom being a far different peace
from the peace of the religion, or spiritual worship, maintained and professed of the citizens.

"Hence it is that so many glorious and flourishing cities of
the world maintain their civil peace; yea, the very Americans
and wildest pagans keep the peace of their towns or cities,
though neither in one nor the other can any man prove a true
church of God in those places, and consequently no spiritual
and heavenly peace." [25]

When, in 1644, Roger Williams secured a charter for Rhode
Island, he was enabled to perform a bold experiment in providing for equality in religious freedom. In the code of law
drafted by the first legislative assembly in the colony, assurance
was given that "all men may walk as their consciences persuade
them, every one in the name of his God." [26] A few years later,
when Williams was seeking a new charter for Rhode Island,
he wrote to his agent in England, John Clarke, "Plead our
cause in such sort as we may not be compelled to exercise
any civil power over men's consciences." And later still, in his
successful appeal to Charles II for a charter, Williams wrote,
"It is much in our hearts to hold forth a lively experiment, that
a most flourishing civil State may stand and best be maintained,
with a full liberty of religious concernments." [27] Rhode Island
left proof through its experience that the practical consequences of a public policy of religious liberty were as conducive to peace as Roger Williams had predicted they would
be.

However, in addition to his views on the separation of church
and state, Williams left another legacy which was equally
important. For Williams was an early advocate of democracy.
The "Sovereign, original, and foundation of civil power lies
in the people," he had written. "And if so . . . a People may
erect and establish what form of Government seems to them

most meet for their civil condition: it is evident that such Governments as are by them erected and established, have no more power, nor for no longer time, than the civil power or people consenting and agreeing shall betrust them with." [28] The preamble to the charter of Rhode Island of 1644 declared that the form of government was to be a democracy, "that is to say, A government held by the free and voluntary consent of all, or the greater part, of the free inhabitants." [29] What remained to be seen subsequently in America was whether the principle of equality of religious freedom, as a right of all inhabitants, would prove compatible with the democratic principle of majority rule.

In the century which lay between the English Toleration Act of 1689 and the Constitution of the United States it seemed evident that the democratic impulse and the drive toward religious freedom were mutually supportive movements. In spite of the unfortunate behavior of the Puritans under Cromwell during the Civil War, it is generally true that it had been the theoretically popular branch of the government which had pressed for liberties against the reluctant Stuart kings. And, for all the restrictiveness of the Toleration Act, with its requirements for the registration of dissenting Protestant ministers, its disqualification of dissenters from public office, and clear discriminations against Catholics, Unitarians, and Jews, it nevertheless marked a decided victory in the struggle for religious liberty. At the time of the Revolution the association of church and state, of bishop and king, seemed to reflect the conditions of the past, while popular liberty including religious freedom suggested the prospects for the future. Because of the organizational structure of the Anglican church, American independence from England meant a separation from bishop as well as king.

In still another way did the movement for national independence promote the cause of independence of the churches in the colonies. The course of the previous century's immigration into the colonies had caused then, as it would later, a considerable displacement in the religious power structure of America. Contented, dedicated Anglicans, it would appear, were not eager to colonize; as a result, they became a minority themselves in most of the colonies. Popular government in the colonies became, therefore, increasingly associated with Protestant dissenters. Once again there seemed to be a necessary association of popular government with religious heterodoxy.

The Revolutionary argument of "no taxation without representation" had its religious counterpart in the protest against taxes imposed in the colonies to maintain religious establishments, in which the issue was a fundamental disagreement over doctrine rather than representation. It was one thing for a colony to impose a tax to support an established church when it was presumed that the church represented the views of the majority; however, it was clearly insufferable to those not of the faith when they constituted a majority to be taxed to support views that they did not endorse.

The displacement in public power brought by more than a century of prosperous economic growth and fostered by a continuing influx of immigrants, that culminated in the political movement for independence, was reflected in the demands of the various religious dissenters for religious independence and freedom. The association of Anglicanism with monarchy was as inevitable as the association of Catholicism with the papacy. The politics of religious association therefore worked against both of these religions on the grounds of nationalism and democracy. For reasons of nationalism, Anglicans were suspected of Tory loyalty, as Catholics were feared by Protestants to have sympathies with Catholic France or Spain. For reasons of democracy, both churches were suspect, because they maintained hierarchical organizations in which office was held by virtue of appointment from above rather than by election from church members. As a result, Catholics were not put on an equal footing with, say, Presbyterians in the early state constitutions, and only the Anglican church was seriously affected by disestablishmentarianism.

For all the evident association of religious freedom with the political power of competing religious groups, the movement toward liberality of belief went well beyond the necessities of power. As democratic sentiment was marshaled to remove previously established religious restrictions, it was evident in the late eighteenth century that religious liberty was consistent with and supported by democratic sentiment. Indeed, in the Bill of Rights of the Virginia Constitution of 1776 the last enumerated right was declared to be: "That religion, or the duty which we owe to our Creator, and the manner of discharging it, can be directed only by reason and conviction, not by force or violence; and therefore all men are equally entitled to the free exercise of religion, according to the dictates of conscience; and that it is the mutual duty of all to practice Christian forbearance, love, and charity towards each other." [30] In 1786, Jefferson's famous bill for Establishing Religious Freedom was enacted into law, bringing about equal rights in religion in Virginia.

In 1787 the Continental Congress passed the Northwest Ordinance which, besides encouraging a public school system in the territory, provided that "No person, demeaning himself in a peaceable and orderly manner, shall ever be molested on account of his mode of worship, or religious sentiments, in the said territory." Soon thereafter the Constitution went into effect, with its highly significant Article Six providing that "No religious Test shall ever be required as a Qualification to any office or public Trust under the United States." There was apparently scant discussion over this article. In 1790 President Washington visited Newport, Rhode Island, and replying to the welcome extended him there by the Touro Synagogue, he observed:

The citizens of the United States of America have the right to applaud themselves for having given to mankind examples of an enlarged and liberal policy worthy of imitation. All possess alike liberty of conscience and immunities of citizenship. It is now no more that toleration is spoken of as if it were by the indulgence of one class of people that another enjoyed the exercise of their inherent natural rights, for happily the Government of the United States, which gives to bigotry no sanction, to persecution no assistance, requires only that they who live under its protection should demean themselves as good citizens in giving it on all occasions their effectual support.[31]

This image of America as a land of equal religious freedom was also fostered by an article intended for potential immigrants, written in 1790 by Hamilton's Assistant Secretary of the Treasury, Tench Coxe. "In this land of promise for the good men of all denominations," he wrote, "are actually to be found the independent or Congregational Church from England, the Protestant Episcopal Church (separated by our Revolution from the Church of England), the Quaker Church, the English, Scotch, Irish and Dutch Presbyterian or Calvinist Churches, the Roman Catholic Church, the German Lutheran Church, the Baptist and Anabaptist Churches, the Huguenot or French Protestant Church, the seceders from the Scotch Church, the Menomist Church, with other Christian sects, and the Hebrew Church. Mere toleration is a doctrine exploded by our general constitution. . . ."[32]

The very variety and multiplicity of sects and denominations which were to threaten the remaining religious establishments in some of the states seemed to assure the promise of an ever widening area of religious freedom. The growth of democracy, paralleling the growth of religious diversity, worked to enlarge the area of religious liberty. So a classic theory of religious liberty developed. A diversity of sects, spread over a wide geographic political area, would find coalition difficult; therefore they would tend to check each other in their conflicting claims to authority. "In a free government," *Federalist* number 51 declared, "the security for civil rights must be the same as that for religious rights. It consists in the one case in the multiplicity of interests, and in the other in the multiplicity of sects. The degree of security in both cases will depend on the number of interests and sects; and this may be presumed to depend on the extent of country and number of people comprehended under the same government." This theory was well illustrated by the constitution itself, with its liberal Article Six. This settlement went beyond the constitutions of most of the states in which the religious pressures were more homogeneous, more insistent, and more easily organized. In 1791 the First Amendment added to the Constitution its vital injunction, "Congress shall make no law respecting an establishment of religion, or prohibiting the free exercise thereof. . . ." The First Amendment completed in constitutional law what may be called here the classic settlement of equal religious freedom, with its distinct separation of church and state.

Over the next half century the various state constitutions were rewritten when necessary to bring them into accord with the national policy, whereby religious freedom was, in effect, if not in exact words, guaranteed equally to all. The course of majority rule through this period had consistently been toward the removal of religious restraints and legal discriminations. In accordance with the classic theory, the majority represented a coalition of jealous sectarians, each distrustful or at least wary of the possibilities of power exercised by the others. It was thus the continued vigilance and jealousy of each opposing sect which worked politically toward the equal freedom for all.

Another impulse hastening the spread of religious freedom during the formative years of the republic came from the Enlightenment, with its philosophical emphasis on mundane causation and mundane solutions. The supernatural explanations of phenomena which had so engaged many of the early Puritans were now reduced philosophically to the category of superstition. Men, such as Jefferson himself, were increasingly concerned with problems of farming, house construction, indeed commonwealth construction, and with all the elaborate gadgetry of a mechanical science which followed in the wake of Newtonian physics. Learned men could, with Jefferson, declare Bacon, Newton, and Locke to be the greatest men in history, thereby disregarding Calvin, Luther, or other great religious figures; or, again with Jefferson, they could deprecate the effect of opposing religious views on the grounds "it neither picks my pocket nor breaks my leg." In all, the Enlightenment manifested a growing concern with the natural as opposed to the supernatural, the here and now as opposed to the hereafter, and material abundance as opposed to spiritual rectitude. Economic communion tended in many areas to become more important than religious communion, and the over-all effect was to make religious differences less significant. This growth of the economic community at the expense of the religious is vividly seen in the *Letters From An American Farmer* (1782) written by Hector St. John de Crèvecoeur just before the Revolution.

Let us suppose you and I to be traveling; we observe that in this house, to the right, lives a Catholic, who prays to God as he has been taught, and believes in transubstantiation; he works and raises wheat, he has a large family of children, all hale and robust; his belief, his prayers offend nobody. About one mile farther on the same road, his next neighbor may be a good honest plodding German Lutheran, who addresses himself to the same God, the God of all, agreeably to the modes he has been educated in, and believes in consubstantiation; by so doing he scandalizes nobody; he also works in his fields, embellishes the earth, clears swamps, etc. What has the world to do with his Lutheran principles? He persecutes nobody, and nobody persecutes him, he visits his neighbors, and his neighbors visit him. Next to him lives a seceder, the most enthusiastic of all sectaries; his zeal is hot and fiery, but separated as he is from others of the same complexion, he has no congregation of his own to resort to, where he might cabal and mingle religious pride with worldly obstinacy. He likewise raises good crops, his house is handsomely painted, his orchard is one of the fairest in the neighborhood. How does it concern the welfare of the country, or of the province at large, what this man's religious sentiments are, or really whether he has any at all? He is a good farmer, he is a sober, peaceable, good citizen: William Penn himself would not wish for more. . . . Next again lives a Low Dutchman, who implicitly believes the rules laid down by the synod of Dort. . . . You will find his house and farm to be the neatest in all the country; and you will judge by his wagon and fat horses, that he thinks more of the affairs of this world than of those of the next. He is sober and laborious, therefore he is all he ought to be as to the affairs of this life; as for those of the next, he must trust to the great Creator. Each of these people instruct their children as well as they can, but these instructions are feeble

compared to those which are given to the youth of the poorest
class in Europe. Their children will therefore grow up less zealous
and more indifferent in matters of religion than their parents. The
foolish vanity, or rather the fury of making Proselytes, is unknown
here; they have no time, the seasons call for all their attention, and
thus in a few years this mixed neighborhood will exhibit a strange
religious medley, that will be neither pure Catholicism nor pure
Calvinism. A very perceptible indifference even in the first generation, will become apparent; and it may happen that the daughter of
the Catholic will marry the son of the seceder, and settle by themselves at a distance from their parents. What religious education
will they give their children? . . . Thus all sects are mixed as well
as all nations; thus religious indifference is imperceptibly dissemi-
nated from one end of the continent to the other; which is at
present one of the strongest characteristics of the Americans. Persecution, religious pride, the love of contradiction, are the food of
what the world commonly calls religion. These motives have
ceased here; zeal in Europe is confined; here it evaporates in the
great distance it has to travel; there it is a grain of powder inclosed,
here it burns away in the open air, and consumes without effect.
. . .[33]

❋

The classic theory of religious liberty in America held that
three factors would work to perpetuate the system. First, constitutional safeguards, both state and national, would guarantee
religious freedom to all and guard the area of religion from
political intervention; the state as well as national governments
would therefore be restricted to a passively neutral role in the
conflicts over religion. Second, religious freedom would in
fact produce a continuing political check in that religions
would continue to grow and sects to multiply; their mutual
jealousy would be the most certain safeguard against the effort
of any one religion to gain political advantage. This was usually
coupled with the theory of continental dilution and diffusion
which assumed that the country was so vast that an effective
coalition of religious interests could not be achieved. This was
the same reasoning that Madison used in *Federalist* number 10

to argue the desirability of the federal system as a check on the evils of factionalism. Finally, it was assumed that the spread of education and the creation of an enlightened citizenry would erase the causes of religious prejudice as well as the forms of bigotry. Thus the benefits of religious freedom equally enjoyed by all would be equally sustained by all, and democracy would prove the best safeguard of religious liberty.

Over the next century there occurred several significant developments which the classic theorists could not have anticipated. The theory, for all of its claimed universality, was at bottom a Protestant solution to what was essentially a Protestant problem: that is, the multiplicity of sects within the Protestant camp. It was drawn up at a time when what might be called the Protestant establishment was the unquestioned religious center of the colonial community. The theory was therefore offered as a solution to the vexing question of how conflicting Protestant sects could live together in peace. Because it also provided a more general answer to how all religious minorities, individual Protestant sects, Catholics, and Jews might so live, it was generally supported by all religious groups. However, it has been estimated that there were probably not over two or three thousand Jews in America at the time of the Revolution out of a colonial population of approximately three million; while the Catholic population has been estimated at approximately three hundred thousand.[34] It would appear therefore reasonable to believe that the inarticulate assumption of such classic theorists as Madison and Jefferson was that they were dealing with a Protestant America.

What has put the theory to its severest test has been the immigration in the nineteenth and twentieth centuries which has brought millions of Catholics and Jews to America. Today it has been estimated that some six million Jews, approximately half the population of Jews in the world, live in the United States;[35] while Catholics, numbering approximately some thirty million, have made the Catholic Church in the United States one of the most formidable bastions of their faith anywhere in the world. The result has been that the classic theory, initially intended to accommodate religious differences primarily among Protestants, must now serve the comprehensive goal of accommodating Protestants, Catholics, and Jews.[36]

A second consequence of immigration was to associate religious differences with social distinctions. Anti-Semitism and anti-Catholicism were early imported into America from the Old World. The early immigrants of course brought over their prejudices. Jefferson, in 1818, expressed his awareness of anti-Semitism in a letter written to Rabbi Mordecai Noah of New York.

Your sect by its sufferings, has furnished a remarkable proof of the universal spirit of religious intolerance inherent in every sect, disclaimed by all while feeble, and practiced by all when in power: Our laws have applied the only antidote to the vice, protecting our religious as they do our civil rights, by putting all men on an equal footing. But more remains to be done; for although we are free by the law, we are not so in practice; public opinion erects itself into an inquisition, and exercises its office with as much fanaticism as fans the flames of an auto de fé: The prejudice still scowling on your section of our religion, although the elder one, cannot be unfelt by yourselves; it is to be hoped that individual dispositions will at length mold themselves to the model of the law, and consider the moral basis on which all our religions rest as the rallying point which unites them in a common interest; while the peculiar dogmas branching from it are the exclusive concern of the respective sects embracing them, and no rightful subject of notice to any other.[37]

The social prejudice against Jews in what was frequently alleged to be a Christian, if not in fact a Protestant, country put Jews politically in a disadvantageous competitive position in protecting their equal religious rights.

The Protestant social prejudice against Catholics continued well after the legal disabilities against them were removed. Alexis de Tocqueville, a Catholic, took his notes for *Democracy In America* (1835) just before a storm of anti-Catholicism broke out. At that time, he noted, there were more than a million Catholics in the country, and priests and laity alike "attributed the peaceful dominion of religion in their country to the separation of Church and State." [38] He found that the spread of democracy had not diminished the role of religion in society as he had feared, but had on the contrary strengthened it by removing religion from politics. And he wrote, "no class of men are more naturally disposed than the Catholics to transfuse the doctrine of the equality of conditions into the political world. . . . Most of the Catholics are poor, and they have no chance of taking a part in the Government unless it be open to all the citizens. They constitute a minority, and all rights must be respected in order to insure to them the free exercise of their own privileges. These two causes induce them, unconsciously to adopt political doctrines which they would perhaps support with less zeal if they were rich and pre-ponderant." [39]

The economic circumstances which the immigrants of 1830 found were, of course, considerably different from those prevailing in America prior to the Revolution. Viewed chronologically, the waves of immigration to America gave Protestants first opportunities, Catholics second, and Jews third. This meant that in many instances after the Revolution succeeding waves of immigrants of necessity took employment in menial occupations. The early master-servant, employer-employee relationship was thus not infrequently a Protestant-Catholic one. In effect, a temporary social and economic distinction was easily confounded with a religious one as a result of latter day immigration, a confusion which was exploited in the anti-Catholic literature of the "Know-Nothings" of the 1850's. From the 1830's until the Civil War an intense wave of anti-Catholicism swept America and made it difficult for Catholics to defend their equal religious rights. The invidious distinction between native American and alien or foreigner at that time usually was applied by Protestants against Catholic immigrants. Catholics were frequently charged with having given their primary allegiance to a foreign power, the pope, a charge popularized by the inventor of the telegraph, Samuel F. B. Morse, in *Foreign Conspiracy Against the Liberties of the*

United States (1835). Jews, nearly a century later, were also to be charged by the bigots with being subservient to a foreign power, the mythical Elders of Zion. The implication in both cases was the same: to be Catholic or Jewish in Protestant America was to be either un-American, or less American than those of native-born Protestant stock.

For various reasons nineteenth and twentieth century Catholic and Jewish immigrants tended to settle in urban areas. City life had been suspect in America since at least the days when Jefferson had penned his classic words on the subject in his *Notes on Virginia;* with the influx of those deemed foreign in religion as well as in national origin, cities became even more suspect. Furthermore, with the rise of political city bosses, and their patronage, the politics of religion often became for immigrants of vital importance for employment, if not for survival. This meant that religion became part and parcel of the already infinitely complex problems of city government. And it meant ultimately that the precarious urban-rural balance in state politics would be further disturbed by the sometimes opposing publics of Protestants, Catholics, and Jews.

It had been assumed in the classic American theory of religious liberty that the strength of conflicting religious forces would be diluted because of their diffusion throughout a vast continent. The opportunities for concerted action would be slight, and the likelihood of agreement on a course of action which would turn public policy to religious advantage most remote. It could hardly have occurred to these early theorists that out of the multiplicity of faiths would come successful coalitions, nor that so many Catholics and Jews would remain voluntarily confined within half a dozen major urban complexes where levels of tension and suspicion were bound to be high. It is however in these cities that the issues of birth control, movie censorship, prayers in public schools, tax exemption of church properties, tax support for parochial schools, and "released time" programs have taken on the most vital political urgency.

Another modern development which has had its impact on

the classic theory has been the tendency to nationalize settlements involving political-religious questions. Many forces have brought this situation about, but only two of them need be noted here. First, problems that were considered purely local in Jefferson's day have inevitably assumed statewide or national importance today. The responsibility for education and welfare programs, once primarily the concern of the churches or local government, has in many instances necessarily been assumed by the national and state governments. And in a larger sense the equal rights of individuals have become nationally guaranteed. Thus the Supreme Court in subsuming the content of the First Amendment under that of the Fourteenth has nationalized religious freedom, a freedom once determined separately by the constitutions of the various states. Second, and closely related to the above, the Supreme Court has become in effect the legal guardian and arbiter of these rights. It has been left to the Court to preserve the views of Jefferson and Madison in our modern complex society. Such a development would have been, it is safe to hazard, inconceivable to Thomas Jefferson.

But more than this. In the absence of a socially accepted established church the Supreme Court has become the moral censor in our society. Its decisions are not only legally binding, but its opinions have all the normative weight which in other societies would be accorded to canon law and the resolutions of church councils. It must in the name of the Constitution articulate the silences in that document. Possessing both authority and sanctity, it has become the supreme spokesman for the values of society which transcend both self-interest and current politics. At no time previously in the history of the court has the issue of equal liberty in religious belief, or disbelief, been of such a vital concern in American jurisprudence as it is today. With over 250 religious organizations competing for liberty and converts, the task of preserving an equality of freedom has proven sufficient to challenge the patience of Job as well as the wisdom of Solomon. It is a tribute to the Supreme Court of this era that the most profound dialogue in contemporary American political thought on the vital issues of religious liberty and political obligation is found in its opinions.[40] These thorny issues, so vitally affecting the rights of all, have had to be decided by men who are themselves privately Protestants, Catholics, and Jews, and who cannot be unmindful of the consequences of their decisions on believers and nonbelievers alike. In the classic words of Justice Frankfurter, however, "as Judges we are neither Jew nor Gentile, neither Catholic nor agnostic. We owe equal attachment to the Constitution and are equally bound by our judicial obligations whether we derive our citizenship from the earliest or the latest immigrants to these shores." [41]

Because the Supreme Court must inevitably deal with the most fundamental moral questions of our social existence, its decisions, while legally binding, cannot finally settle problems in a democracy; the court can only return its answers in the form of instructive opinions to the national community where the consciences of men must make the ultimate choice. Again, to quote Justice Frankfurter:

Judicial review, itself a limitation on popular government, is a fundamental part of our constitutional scheme. But to the legislature no less than to courts is committed the guardianship of deeply-cherished liberties. . . . Where all the effective means of inducing political changes are left free from interference, education in the abandonment of foolish legislation is itself a training in liberty. To fight out the wise use of legislative authority in the forum of public opinion and before legislative assemblies rather than to transfer such a contest to the judicial arena, serves to vindicate the self-confidence of a free people.[42]

❋

Fundamentally, therefore, the problem of preserving the classic settlement of equal religious liberty in the modern environment becomes essentially one of education. This poses an obvious difficulty, for it is precisely over the public policy in education that the most intense religious disputes take place today. "Two great drives," Mr. Justice Rutledge observed nearly two decades ago, "are constantly in motion to abridge, in the name of education, the complete division of religion and civil authority which our forefathers made. One is to introduce religious education and observances into the public schools. The other, to obtain funds for the aid and support of various private religious schools." [43] Neither of these drives has diminished in strength since those lines were written; nor are the challenges they present at all novel. Essentially, Americans have always had to reconcile politically two logically opposing principles. On the one hand, the role of conscience to determine the proper relationship of man to God has been held to be the most vital and sacred immunity a man holds in society; on the other hand, the right of society to set the terms and conditions of public peace is unquestioned. It was a dilemma not unknown to Roger Williams over three hundred years ago when he took the stand in his famous letter to the town of Providence (1655) that the claim to immunities because of religious belief could not relieve one of public obligations in the ship of state.

If any of the seamen refuse to perform their services, or passengers to pay their freight; if any refuse to help, in person or purse, towards the common charges or defence; if any refuse to obey the common laws and orders of the ship, concerning their common peace or preservation; if any shall mutiny and rise up against their commanders or officers, because all are equal in Christ, therefore no masters nor officers, no laws nor orders, nor corrections nor punishments;—I say, I never deemed, but in such cases, whatever is pretended, the commander or commanders may judge, resist, compel and punish such transgressions, according to their deserts and merits.[44]

Or, to state the matter in the words of Mr. Justice Frankfurter in the first flag salute case (subsequently overruled), "The mere possession of religious convictions which contradict the relevant concerns of a political society does not relieve the citizen from the discharge of political responsibilities." [45] And again his dissent in the subsequent flag salute case, "The constitutional protection of religious freedom terminated disabilities, it did not create new privileges. It gave religious equality, not civil immunity." [46] As a matter of fact, however, in our efforts to reconcile the conflicts of religious immunity and public policy we have frequently made exceptions in general policy on a pragmatic basis when it has been felt that the consequences of such exceptions would not threaten the peace and security of the nation. These exceptions for the few are made possible precisely because they are not indulged in by the many. Clearly the Quaker exception to bearing arms, which would certainly have been precluded in principle by the statements of both Williams and Frankfurter, is possible only because the great majority of eligible adult males do not claim this immunity of conscientious objection during a draft call. Were all Presbyterians or Catholics or Baptists to claim it, then this pragmatic solution to the problem of national security would be doubtless subjected to further reconsideration.

A more acute problem arises with the effort to introduce or perpetuate religious ritual, doctrine, or liturgy into the public schools, either by direct or indirect means. It may be assumed that Mr. Justice Douglas's assertion that "We are a religious people whose institutions presuppose a Supreme Being," was a statement of fact rather than a binding conclusion in law.[47] But the fundamental problem now, as in the past, is how may even a religious people of diverse religions live together in temporal peace? It would be well if the compulsions of religious charity led to a golden rule of politics by which the majority would not do in the name of its most cherished beliefs that which it would not have done to it were it unalterably opposed to these tenets and in a clear minority. Proselytizing, however, seems to be as much a part of religion as prayer, and the temptation to draw the sanction of the state into play has proven all too frequently irresistible. When religion enters into politics, it leaves the spiritual world for the temporal realm where there are fears and jealousies and considerations of power.

In the light of the American classic theory of separation of church and state the effort to invoke the authority of the teacher in prayers in public schools or the truant officer in "released-time" catechism is clearly unwise, not only because it confounds the spiritual and temporal but because it subjects the community to a needless source of conflict. The effort to make uniform any aspect of individual conscience in religion by a compulsory public education system must produce in some measure the untoward consequences which the classic American belief in the separation of church and state intended to avoid. "If there is any fixed star in our constitutional constellation," Mr. Justice Jackson has observed, "it is that no official, high or petty, can prescribe what shall be orthodox in politics, nationalism, religion, or other matters of opinion or force citizens to confess by word or act their faith therein." [48] And in his dissent in the released-time case of *Zorach v. Clauson* (1952) he further observed, "The day that this country ceases to be free for irreligion it will cease to be free for religion." The same point was made in dissent in the same case by Mr. Justice Black: "The First Amendment has lost much if the religious follower and the atheist are no longer to be judicially regarded as entitled to equal justice under law." [49] The mere presence of 256 organized religious bodies in the United States must suggest the possibility of at least 257 answers to fundamental theological questions. Every effort by any of these groups to further its creed through political action must stimulate in its opponents a responding political demand. The practical result of such a continuous contest must be to turn the public schools into the political pawns of a religious power struggle in which the equality of men in religious freedom would be certainly placed in jeopardy.

A similar situation is presented by the pressure to utilize public funds in aid of church schools. A church school draws its reason for existence from the desire of its supporters to inculcate students with the tenets of that particular church. It is indeed an establishment of religion in the sense that that term is used in the First Amendment. Mr. Justice Black, speaking for the majority in the controversial decision of *Everson v. Board of Education* (1947), which upheld the reimbursement to parents of money spent on bus transportation of their children to Catholic parochial schools, declared:

The 'establishment of religion' clause of the First Amendment means at least this: Neither a state nor the Federal Government can set up a church. Neither can pass laws which aid one religion, aid all religions, or prefer one religion over another. Neither can force nor influence a person to go to or to remain away from church against his will or force him to profess a belief or disbelief in any religion. No person can be punished for entertaining or professing religious beliefs or disbeliefs, for church attendance or non-attendance. No tax in any amount, large or small, can be levied to support any religious activities or institutions, whatever they may be called, or whatever form they may adopt to teach or practice religion. . . . In the words of Jefferson, the clause against establishment of religion by law was intended to erect 'a wall of separation between Church and State'.[50]

It is, however, not alone the constitutional argument but the classic theory behind it which precludes the use of public funds for church schools. To increase the stakes of religious controversy by putting public funds in the pot is only to feed the fires of religious controversy by making in effect public, and therefore subject to majority rule, that which in its final analysis is intrinsically a private affair.[51] Such a violation of church and state ultimately makes the church subservient to the state, dependent upon it not only for funds but eventually for approval of doctrine. Madison, in his classic *Remonstrance Against a Bill Establishing a Provision for Teachers of the Christian Religion in Virginia* (cited by both sides in the Everson case), cautioned that "it is proper to take alarm at the first experiment on our liberties. We hold this prudent jealousy to be the first duty of citizens. . . . Who does not see that the same authority which can establish Christianity, in exclusion of all other Religions, may establish with the same ease any particular sect of Christians, in exclusion of all other Sects? That the same authority which can force a citizen to contribute three pence only of his property for the support of any one establishment, may force him to conform to any other establishment in all cases whatsoever?" [52]

A "prudent jealousy" of a free people would require that

the subject matter of religious belief or disbelief remain, in accordance with the classic settlement, forever beyond the reach of governmental authority. No other right which men may lay claim to is as sacred, whether considered theologically or philosophically, as the right to seek out the answers in that realm of mystery which has throughout history challenged the essential unity of humanity with the diversity of man's belief. In an age in which the necessities of our temporal interdependence must inexorably invade the privacy of the self, the last yet most noble refuge of the self remains the individual conscience. That which gives strength and depth and character to conscience is not the compulsion of society, whether given in the form of approval or coercion, but the opportunities for growth, for creativity, for contemplation; for, in effect, making daily the ultimate decisions. In this, all men are equally challenged; in this lies our fundamental equality.

Yet this only poses again the fundamental dilemma of how conscientious men, each firmly convinced of the rightness of his convictions, can live in peace with their neighbors of opposing and militant religious views. The convictions of conscience, to be meaningful, must eventually be translated into actions which affect other men. The American experience of religious conflict has given ample testimony that an appeal to conscience to restrain the social actions impelled by conscience is a most inadequate safeguard for religious liberty. Paradoxically, the surest safeguard for the equal exercise of religious liberty has not rested in an appeal to religious principles but in the diffusion of religious power. This was the safeguard anticipated by those worldly philosophers who formulated the classic settlement, seeing in the problem of power the essentials of the problem of freedom and maintaining the price of freedom to be "prudent jealousy" and "eternal vigilance." The modern developments, discussed above, by focusing attention on religious conflict have actually reinforced the classic settlement. The awareness that power and freedom are politically associated has thus worked to continue that basic equality of religious freedom in which no religion is so powerful as to be completely free and no religion so subjugated as to be without power. It is in this second-best solution to the problem of power that we have achieved what our experience has vindicated as the best solution to the problem of religious freedom.

NOTES

1. John Calvin, *Institutes of the Christian Religion,* translated by J. Allen (Philadelphia: Presbyterian Board of Christian Education, 7th American edition, 1936), Vol. II, p. 772.
2. Stephen Junius Brutus, *A Defense of Liberty Against Tyrants* (1579; trans. anon., 1648), in William Ebenstein, *Great Political Thinkers* (New York: Rinehart and Co., 1951), p. 321.
3. Robert Cardinal Bellarmine, *On the Power of the Supreme Pontiff in Temporal Matters,* in William Y. Elliott and Neil A. McDonald, *Western Political Heritage* (Englewood Cliffs, N.J.: Prentice-Hall, Inc., 1949), p. 409.
4. Ola Elizabeth Winslow, *Master Roger Williams* (New York: Macmillan Company, 1957), p. 70.
5. John Cotton, *The Way of the Congregational Churches Cleared,* cited in Thomas J. Wertenbaker, *The Puritan Oligarchy* (New York: Charles Scribner's Sons, 1947), p. 23.
6. John Locke, *Letter Concerning Toleration,* in Elliott and McDonald, *op. cit.,* p. 412.
7. Nathaniel Ward, *The Simple Cobbler of Aggawam,* quoted in Perry Miller and Thomas H. Johnson, *The Puritans* (New York: American Book Co., 1938), p. 227.
8. Winslow, *op. cit.,* p. 198.
9. Roger Williams, *The Bloody Tenent of Persecution* (London: J. Haddon, 1848), p. 20.
10. *Ibid.,* pp. 1–2.
11. *Ibid.,* p. 33.
12. *Ibid.,* pp. 46–7.
13. Sanford H. Cobb, *The Rise of Religious Liberty In America* (New York: Macmillan Company, 1902), p. 97.
14. *Ibid.,* p. 207–8.
15. *Ibid.,* p. 68.
16. *Ibid.,* p. 206.
17. Anson Phelps Stokes, *Church and State in the United States* (New York: Harper and Brothers, 1950), Vol. I, pp. 189–90.
18. *Ibid.,* p. 190.

19. *Ibid.*, p. 192.
20. Cobb, *op. cit.*, p. 441.
21. *Ibid.*, p. 443.
22. Evarts B. Greene, *Religion and the State* (New York: New York University Press, 1941), p. 58.
23. Stokes, *op. cit.*, Vol. I, p. 208.
24. Williams, *op. cit.*, p. 9.
25. *Ibid.*, p. 46.
26. Cobb, *op. cit.*, p. 431.
27. *Ibid.*, p. 435.
28. Roger Williams, "The Bloody Tenet," *Narragansett Club Publications* (Providence, 1866–70), Vol. III, pp. 249–50.
29. Cobb, *op. cit.*, p. 28.
30. Francis N. Thorpe, *The Federal and State Constitutions* (Washington: U.S. Government Printing Office, 1909), Vol. VII, p. 3814.
31. Stokes, *op. cit.*, Vol. I, p. 862.
32. Gustavus Myers, *History of Bigotry in the United States* (New York: Random House, Inc., 1943), p. 113.
33. Hector St. John de Crèvecoeur, *Letters from an American Farmer* (London: Thomas Davis, 1782), pp. 59–63.
34. Howard M. Sachar, *The Course of Modern Jewish History* (Cleveland: The World Publishing Co., 1958), p. 162. William W. Sweet, *The American Churches: An Interpretation* (New York: Abingdon-Cokesbury Press, 1948), p. 93.
35. Jacob Lestschinsky, "Jewish Migrations, 1840–1946" in *The Jews: Their History, Culture, Religion* (New York: Harper and Brothers, 1949), Vol. II, p. 1221.
36. Some of the difficulties of this accommodation may be seen in the following editorials: "To Our Jewish Friends," *America*, Sept. 1, 1962, pp. 665–6; "The Main Issue," *America*, Sept. 15, 1962, p. 713; "On Warning Jews," *The Commonweal*, Sept. 7, 1962, pp. 483–4; "Is *America* Trying To Bully the Jews," *The Christian Century*, Sept. 5, 1962, pp. 1057–8.
37. Stokes, *op. cit.*, Vol. I, pp. 862–3.
38. Alexis de Tocquerville, *Democracy in America* (New York: Oxford University Press, 1947), p. 203.
39. *Ibid.*, p. 197.
40. See especially: *Minersville School District v. Gobitis*, 310 US 586 (1940); *West Virginia State Board of Education v. Barnette*, 319 US 624 (1943); *Everson v. Board of Education*, 330 US 1 (1947); *Illinois ex. rel. McCollum v. Board of Education*, 333 US 203 (1948); *Zorach v. Clauson*, 343 US 306 (1952); *Engel v. Vitale*, 8 L ed 2d 601 (1962).
41. 319 US 647.
42. 310 US 600.

43. 330 US 63.

44. John Russell Bartlett (ed.), "Letters of Roger Williams, 1632–1682," *Publications of the Narragansett Club* (Providence: 1874), Vol. VI, pp. 278–9.

45. 310 US 594–5.

46. 319 US 653.

47. 343 US 313.

48. 319 US 642.

49. 343 US 325, 320.

50. 330 US 15–16.

51. Justice Douglas, in *Engel v. Vitale*, 8 L ed 2d 616, observed that "once government finances a religious exercise it inserts a divisive influence into our communities."

52. 330 US 65–6.

2 RACE

THE AMICABLE accommodation of religious differences in America has been a significant achievement of our political experience; our inability to achieve a similar accommodation of racial differences has been our most conspicuous political failure. At the outset certain obvious differences between the issue of religion and race which help indicate the complexity of the problems of race should be noted. Issues of religion are essentially private and voluntary; issues of race are inevitably conspicuous and involuntary. That is to say, religious conviction, or the lack of it, is contained within the individual; it may indeed never become known but remain a well-kept secret of the soul. Religious conviction does not necessarily appear on sight, as it were, as something to be remarked on.

Furthermore, except that it might be said that the family culture determines the religious beliefs of most children, religious belief is essentially optional and voluntary. Beliefs may thus be kept, changed, or disavowed within the mind of the individual without the world being any whit the wiser. This means that, in effect, the individual may always weigh the consequences of his religious convictions, privately held, against the consequences of a public manifestation of them. They are only volitionally conspicuous. It means also that, when the social price for maintaining an unaccepted belief is too high for an individual in terms of his attachment to that belief, he may change his allegiance to a more socially acceptable creed. Where there is apparent conflict in accommodating religious diversity the first alternative on the part of the individual who is experiencing this conflict is either to hold to his belief or to change his religious allegiance. Thus, not all issues of religious conflict meet head-on, for there is always a certain amount of room for adjustment by those not totally committed.

Issues of race are different. One may not be privately dark-skinned or slant-eyed or of a blond complexion. Race questions occur because race is conspicuous and therefore in public view. And of course, race is involuntary; children may not choose their race when they come of age but, for better or worse, are forever the prisoners of their physiognomy. So there is no leeway for individual accommodation when conflicts of race arise; all clashes are overt and conspicuous. Politically this makes them much more difficult to resolve.

Furthermore, when the early settlers came to America they transplanted the religious disputes they had brought with them, issues which were then a century old. Modern religious conflict, as old at least as the early Reformation, had brought forth decades of experience in trial and error. Racial conflict, an essentially new experience, had hardly begun at the time the classic religious settlement was already established. In time, however, the principle of equality emerged as the only equitable solution to the problem of inevitable diversity of races.

The early English settlers of North America were ill-prepared to cope with the racial diversity which they met with in the New World. Seeking land rather than gold, they came as homesteaders to settle, not as soldiers to conquer. They brought with them their wives, their families, and, to augment the supply of labor, indentured servants. Dependent upon the Indians for neither sex nor labor, the settlers tended to remain aloof from the Indian culture. This aloofness was observed by an eighteenth-century writer, William Byrd of Virginia, who noted of the early settlers that after the initial landing in 1607: "They had now made peace with the Indians, but there was one thing wanting to make that peace lasting. The natives could by no means persuade themselves that the English were heartily their friends, so long as they disdained to intermarry with them. And, in earnest, had the English consulted their own security and the good of the Colony—had they intended either to civilize or convert these gentiles, they would have brought their stomachs to embrace this prudent alliance." Had the early settlers been good Christians, Byrd noted, charity would have dictated that they "take this only method of converting the natives to Christianity. For, after all that can be said, a sprightly lover is the most prevailing missionary that can be sent amongst these, or any other Infidels."

Besides, the poor Indians would have had less reason to complain that the English took away their land, if they had received it by way of portion with their daughters. Had such affinities been contracted in the beginning, how much bloodshed had been prevented, and how populous would the country have been, and, consequently, how considerable? Nor would the shade of the skin have been any reproach at this day; for if a Moor may be washed white in 3 generations, surely an Indian might have been blanched in two.[1]

The social approval of interracial marriages was then, as now, the ultimate test of the acceptance of racial equality in society. The concept of racial inequality has traditionally been based on the claim that physiological traits inherited from a subject race are linked to cultural traits which would reflect a lower stage of civilization than that possessed by the dominant race. As a result, the dominant race tends not only to feel toward those alleged to be racially inferior some measure of emotional revulsion but also to view them as a positive barrier to progress. The racial integrity of the dominant race is regarded as essential to its cultural intactness in the forward march of civilization. Racial exclusiveness of the dominant race is felt to be emotionally desirable as well as morally defensible, and the discriminations which surround the allegedly inferior race are therefore legitimatized.

It was evident to various Indians soon after the settlement in Massachusetts became firmly established that the white colonizers posed an economic threat to Indian existence. For example, it is reported that one chief, Miantunnomoh, spoke to the Long Island chief, Waiandance, and his people (about 1642) as follows: "Brothers, we must be one as the English are, or we shall soon all be destroyed. You know our fathers had plenty of deer and skins, and our plains were full of deer and of turkeys, and our coves and rivers were full of fish. But, brothers, since these English have seized upon our country, they cut down the grass with scythes, and the trees with axes. Their cows and horses eat up the grass, and their hogs spoil our beds of clams; and finally we shall starve to death." [2] This lament over a lost country was voiced increasingly throughout the remainder of the colonial period.

Without an effective political or economic lever to maintain their rights against the white culture, the Indians resorted to force, in which they were of course no match for the whites. "We are born free," Grangula, chief of the Onondagas, declared to the French Governor-General of Canada in 1684. "We neither depend on Yonnondio [governors of Canada] nor Corlear [governors of New York]. We may go where we please, and carry with us whom we please, and buy and sell what we please." [3] They, however, lacked the power to make good their claims. Their state of dependence became such that both the French and the English were able to exploit their services in the French and Indian War, as the Revolutionists and Loyalists were able to exploit them subsequently in the American Revolution.

By the time of the American Revolution it was evident that race consciousness, with invidious distinctions of superiority and inferiority, was becoming increasingly prevalent. A Captain Pipe, chief of the Delawares, reportedly said to the commandant of the British garrison at Detroit, who had called upon the Delawares to fight the Americans, "Who of us can believe that you can love a people of a different color from your own better than those who have a white skin like yourselves?" [4]

From the time that the earliest white settlements were firmly established on the Eastern seaboard until the last cluster of

Indians were gathered on the barren desert reservations of the Southwest, the declining power of the Indians was evidenced by their declining status in the dominant white society. Restrictions on their areas for living, on their economic activity, for decades on their American citizenship, taboos on intermarriage, and an assumption of their racial inferiority were all attendant on their loss of power as they became cultural outcasts in the age of progress.

❋

The problems of racial diversity in early America were further complicated by the importation of Negroes into Virginia in 1619. Some indication of the prevailing attitude of whites toward Negroes in Virginia may be seen in a court record of 1630. "Hugh Davis to be soundly whipt before an assembly of Negroes and others for abusing himself to the dishonor of God and shame of Christianity by defiling his body in lying with a Negro, which fault he is to acknowledge next Sabbath day." [5] By the time that the "self-evident" truth that all men were created equal was proclaimed in the Declaration of Independence there were approximately half a million slaves in America. By 1790, in spite of the opposition to the continuation of the slave trade, this number had increased to approximately 700,000. This number of Negroes (both free and slave) constituted some 19 per cent of the population of the country, the highest ratio of Negroes to whites that has existed in our history. [6] The opposition to the slave trade in the late eighteenth century may be seen as an early effort at racially restricted immigration as well as an antislavery effort prompted by humanitarian principles. In 1772 the Virginia House of Burgesses petitioned the Crown to cease disallowing legislation which checked the slave trade, for: "The importation of slaves into the Colonies from the coast of Africa, hath long been considered as a trade of great inhumanity, and under its present encouragement, we have too much reason to fear will endanger the very existence of your Majesty's American dominions." [7]

After independence, Southern as well as Northern states sought to restrict the foreign slave trade through taxation or to prohibit it altogether. "The records show, however," a student of this subject has written, "that the efforts to abolish or limit the importations of slaves were not prompted by a regard for the rights of man. They were motivated primarily by the fear and the grave danger that the Negroes would become so numerous as to upset the safe ratio of the races and create a social peril and a military menace." [8]

In 1807, Congress enacted the legislation which legally brought the importation of slaves to an end. This legislation marked the end of the 19 per cent Negro-white ratio and indeed the end of any significant Negro immigration into the United States.

The prejudice against Negroes was so strong early in the nineteenth century that, in addition to the prohibition of the further importation of slaves into the country, many of the Northern states had passed laws against the immigration of free Negroes, while in the South removal from the state was often looked upon as a condition of emancipation. Less than a decade after Congress had acted to legally close the foreign slave trade an effort was launched to bring about the settlement of free Negroes outside the United States. In November 1816, a meeting was held in New Jersey to secure signatures to a memorial to the state legislature to "use their influence with the national legislature to adopt some plan of colonizing the 'free blacks'." In December the Virginia House of Delegates, by a vote of 137 to 9, passed a resolution requesting the President to obtain land on the North Pacific Coast for emancipated Negroes. The Virginia Senate later added to the resolution the alternative of the coast of Africa. In Washington, late in December 1816, Henry Clay was chairman of a meeting to encourage the colonization of free Negroes. Finally, in January 1817, a "Memorial of the President and managers of the American society for colonizing the free people of color of the United States" was presented to the House of Representatives (where it was tabled). It stated in part:

It is now reduced to be a maxim, equally approved in philosophy and practice, that the existence of distinct and separate casts and classes, forming exceptions to the general system of polity adapted to the community, is an inherent vice in the composition of society. . . . If this maxim be true in the general, it applies with peculiar force to the relative condition of the free people of color in the United States; between whom and the rest of the community, a combination of causes, political, physical, and moral, has created distinctions, unavoidable in their origin, and most unfortunate in their consequences. . . . The evil has become so apparent and the necessity for a remedy so palpable, that some of the most considerable of the slave-holding states have been induced to impose restraints upon the practice of emancipation, by annexing conditions, which have no effect but to transfer the evil from one state to another. . . .[9]

The "Memorial," signed by Bushrod Washington as president of the society, called upon Congress for assistance in the society's endeavors toward colonization. In 1821, when, after the great debate, Missouri entered the Union, the society purchased land in Liberia to begin its colonization movement. A decade later, in the year that William Lloyd Garrison commenced publication of the *Liberator*, the Society had returned fewer than 1,500 Negroes to Africa. "The real significance of the colonization schemes," Ralph Bunche has observed, "is to be found in the conception of the Negro as an evil that had to be done away with." [10]

White Americans, unable to eliminate racial diversity, were faced with the alternatives of racial equality or white supremacy (with or without slavery); they chose the latter. When, in the debate over the admission of Missouri into the Union, Northerners advanced the equalitarian theory of the Declaration of Independence as precluding the admission of slavery into new states, their Southern opponents chided them with their own inequalitarian practices. "If your humanity has conquered your prejudice, till you know no color," Senator Richard M. Johnson of Kentucky inquired, "where are your magistrates, your governors, your representatives, of the black population?" And Representative Louis McLane of Delaware rhetorically asked, "Where is the State in the Union in which the emancipated negro has been admitted to the enjoyment of equal rights with the white population? I know of none." [11]

It was while the debate on the Missouri question was still raging in 1821, that Thomas Jefferson, 78 years old, wrote his *Autobiography*. In 1779 he had drafted a bill which was to have stopped the importation of slaves into Virginia; he had later drafted a bill for gradual emancipation in Virginia. In his *Autobiography*, he wrote on the Negro question:

Nothing is more certainly written in the book of fate, than that these people are to be free; nor is it less certain that the two races, equally free, cannot live in the same government. Nature, habit, opinion have drawn indelible lines of distinction between them. It is still in our power to direct the process of emancipation and deportation, peaceably, and in such slow degree, as that the evil will wear off insensibly, and their place be, *pari passu*, filled up by free laborers. If, on the contrary, it is left to force itself on, human nature must shudder at the prospect held up.[12]

As late as 1855 an English traveler in the United States, William Chambers, was quoted as having observed, "There seems, in short, to be a fixed notion throughout the whole of the States, whether slave or free, that the colored is by nature a subordinate race; and that in no circumstances, can it be considered equal to the white." [13] This view accorded with the opinion of Abraham Lincoln in his Peoria speech of 1854 when he contemplated the equality of Negroes with whites. "My own feelings will not admit of this," Lincoln declared, "and if mine would, we well know that those of the great mass of whites will not. Whether this feeling accords with justice and sound judgment is not the sole question, if indeed it is any part of it. A universal feeling, whether well or ill founded, cannot be safely disregarded. We cannot then make them equals." [14] Lincoln thus articulated the national assumption of white supremacy.

With the entrance of Missouri into the Union as a slave state the great division over slavery became the paramount political issue which culminated in the Civil War and obscured somewhat the white American consensus. This division did not, however, destroy the early nineteenth century consensus of white superiority.

＊

It is perhaps some testimony to man's rationality that he is reluctant to accept force alone as an adequate basis for authority but seeks to join with force a legitimatizing myth. " 'Might Makes Right' has been, through the ages, sufficient justification for territorial conquest, economic exploitation, and the enslavement of some human groups by others," the anthropologist Juan Comas wrote recently. "In time, however, 'might makes right' ceased to be acceptable, and it was necessary for dominant groups to develop other arguments which would permit them, with a semblance of morality and even of justice, to continue their socio-economic control of great regions of the world." [15] Early in the nineteenth century, modern white racial theory developed as a legitimatizing myth to support the social condition of white superiority achieved through colonialism and slavery.

The close connection between social theory and social condition is clearly seen in the rise of slavery in Southern thought from the status of an "unwanted evil" to that of a "positive good." This change in theory coincided with the rise of cotton as the dominant economic crop in the South. In the decade between the debate on the Missouri Compromise and the opening salvos of the revived abolitionist movement with the publication of Garrison's *Liberator* in 1831 the production of cotton doubled, and this total doubled again by 1840. Slavery, it was said, was essential to the production of cotton. When the abolitionists attacked slavery they were in effect undermining the major prop of the entire Southern social structure.

The legitimatizing myth for slavery, however, had to reach beyond the materialistic argument of economic expediency to the moralistic ground of divine sanction or the deterministic presentations of primitive ethnology, in effect demonstrating the validity of the opinion of the racist writer Dr. Josiah C. Nott that "a man's conscience is always on the side of his interest." [16] The significance of theological and purportedly ethnological arguments in defense of slavery lay not alone in their uses to bring a "higher truth" to the support of the "peculiar institution." The larger applicability of these arguments survived the Civil War to leave a lasting assumption in the minds of some that the races of man were by some law beyond human control inherently and eternally unequal. Although constitutions and statutes might protect or even prohibit slavery, in the long run what was really at issue were those "truths" which might be judged as unalterable by constitutions and statutes, those truths which lay at the core of one's belief in the equality, or inequality, of races. Theology and ethnology thus remained authoritative sources for discussion. [17]

*

The use of race theory to give legitimacy to the superior condition of whites and the subordinate condition of Negroes was a fundamental part of the slavery controversy. It has remained, however, a fundamental part of the segregation controversy, for the subordination of Negroes is as essential to segregation as it was to slavery. The Association of Citizens' Councils draws upon the same essential themes that the proslavery writers drew upon a century ago. For instance, a few months after the school segregation case of *Brown v. Board of Education* was decided in 1954, Reverend G. T. Gillespie gave an address entitled "A Christian View on Segregation" before the Synod of Mississippi of the Presbyterian Church, in which he drew upon the story of Ham to defend segregation.

After the flood the three sons of Noah, Shem, Ham and Japheth, became the progenitors of three distinct racial groups, which were to repeople and overspread the earth. The descendents of Shem migrated eastward and occupied most of Asia; the descendents of

Japheth migrated westward and ultimately occupied the continent of Europe, while the children of Ham moved generally southward toward the tropics and occupied the continent of Africa, and possibly southern Asia and the islands of the Pacific.

This brief record, the accuracy of which has not been successfully disputed by the anthropologists and ethnologists, while affirming the unity of the race, also implies that an all-wise Providence has 'determined the times before appointed, and the bounds of their habitation.' Which same Providence by determining the climatic and other physical conditions under which many successive generations of the several racial groups should live, is thereby equally responsible for the distinct racial characteristics which seem to have become fixed in prehistoric times, and which are chiefly responsible for the segregation of racial groups across the centuries and in our time.[18]

The Reverend Mr. Gillespie then proceeded to explain the Biblical story of the tower of Babel and the confusion of tongues so that, taken with the scattering of peoples, it could be seen as "an act of special Divine Providence to frustrate the mistaken efforts of godless men to assure the permanent integration of the peoples of the earth." Further, he maintained, "the development of different languages was not merely natural or accidental, but served a Divine purpose, in becoming one of the most effective means of preserving the separate existence of the several racial groups." [19]

This view may be compared with that of Dr. Samuel A. Cartwright of New Orleans, who wrote, in 1843, to prove "the truth of the Bible and the justice and benevolence of the decree dooming Canaan to be a servant of servants."

By the discovery of America Japheth became enlarged as had been foretold 3800 years before. He took the whole continent. He literally dwelt in the tents of Shem in Mexico and Central America. No sooner did Japheth begin to enlarge himself, and to dwell in the tents of Shem, than Canaan left his fastnesses in the wilds of Africa, where the white man's foot had never trod, and appeared on the beach to get passage to America, as if drawn thither by an impulse of his nature to fulfill his destiny of becoming Japheth's servant.[20]

In the ante-bellum South one of the most significant race theorists was Dr. Josiah Clark Nott of Mobile, Alabama. It was Dr. Nott's contention that there was "a genus, man, comprising two or more species;" that there had been in fact a plural creation, and Negroes were an inferior species. By 1850 he had so succeeded in producing a scientific as well as a theological debate over his theories that he was able to boast to a friend, "My great object for several years has been to get the world quarreling about niggerology and I have at last succeeded. . . ." [21] While Nott's views on a plural creation had only passing significance, his fundamental views on racial inferiority became widely accepted in his day. On the eve of the Civil War, Chancellor William Harper of South Carolina could solemnly assert, in that massive compilation of pro-slavery thought entitled *Cotton Is King* (1860), "That the African negro is an inferior variety of the human race, is, I think, now generally admitted, and his distinguishing characteristics are such as peculiarly mark him out for the situation which he occupies among us." [22]

Nearly a century later, when the race argument had shifted from slavery to segregation, the belief in Negro inferiority was put forward again. In an address before the Commonwealth Club of California in 1957 a former instructor in sociology at the University of Mississippi, Judge Tom P. Brady, spoke on "Segregation and the South." "Ninety-eight per cent of both races prefer segregation," he declared. "Integration is urged by the NAACP, a few Southern mulattoes, Northern Communist-front organizations and left-wing labor groups who would use the unsuspecting Negro as their tool. It does not work any economic hardship nor deprive the Negro of any of his constitutional rights." [23] The gulf between Negroes and whites, Judge Brady noted, was caused by:

an inherent deficiency in mental ability, of psychological and temperamental inadequacy. It is because of indifference and natural indolence on the part of the Negro. All the races of the earth started out at approximately the same time in God's calendar, but of all the races that have been on this earth, the Negro race is the only race that lacked mental ability and the imagination to put its dreams, hopes and thoughts in writing. The Negro is the only race that was unable to invent even picture writing.[24]

It was a common contention of the proslavery theorists before the Civil War that slavery was a beneficial system of human relationships in that it brought civilization to the slaves. Its legitimacy then rested in part on the benefits it brought to those declared to be subordinate. For instance, Chancellor William Harper argued that most men were averse to labor and, therefore, coercion was as necessary to develop habits of labor as the latter were necessary to the acquisitions of property. "The coercion of slavery alone is adequate to form men to habits of labor." [25] Slavery, as a system of social relationships, was thus seen as a positive good to society.

Approximately a century later, when the issue was segregation rather than slavery, Senator James O. Eastland in an address before a convention of the Association of Citizens' Councils of Mississippi declared: "The institution of segregation has been the primary instrument in the growth, development and progress of the negro race. . . . No similar group of people in known history have made greater strides and advancement in so short a period of time as have the American negro under segregation. The white people have been largely responsible for this progress." [26] Segregation, therefore, was a positive good.

There are many additional parallels between the legitimatizing myth of slavery and the legitimatizing myth of segregation as articulated by the Citizens' Councils. For example, in both instances it was argued that the subject people were happier under the existing arrangement than they would be under any other, that they enjoyed the maximum of freedom compatible with social welfare, and that the beneficial existing arrangements were acceptable to all except a minority of trouble makers from the outside—the abolitionists or the NAACP. In both cases the States' Rights theory was the last resort, and in both a defense of the status quo was associated with the highest principles of conservatism in opposition to an alleged socialism originating in the North.

In 1850 John C. Calhoun observed that: "In this tendency to conflict in the North, between labor and capital, which is constantly on the increase, the weight of the South has and will ever be found on the conservative side. . . ." [27] Slavery provided the institutional matrix for social stability and conservatism. In 1857 George Fitzhugh of Virginia wrote his defense of slavery under the startling title of *Cannibals All* and cheerfully proclaimed "Liberty for the few—Slavery, in every form, for the mass!" In the North liberty and laissez faire had run rampant in society.

> The doctrines so prevalent with Abolitionists and socialists, of Free Love and Free Lands, Free Churches, Free Women and Free Negroes—of No-Marriage, No-Religion, No-Private Property, No-Law and No-Government, are legitimate deductions, if not obvious corollaries from the leading and distinctive axiom of political economy—*Laissez faire*, or let alone.[28]

A century later, in 1957, Judge Tom P. Brady of the Citizens' Council of Mississippi wrote:

> Segregation is but one distinguishing characteristic of the South, it has other attributes. The South is the citadel of conservatism. It is a bastion for constitutional government. For years Mississippi and the entire South have been gravely concerned over the socialist trend of our Federal Government. Beginning with the administration of Franklin D. Roosevelt, the South viewed with alarm the birth of the welfare state, and the growth of the 130 odd Communist-front organizations which nourish it. The South has constantly disapproved the prodigal give-away program to the Communist and socialist countries abroad. It resented the competing by the Federal Government with private industry. It deplored the tolerance shown the Communist and left-wing groups in America.[29]

The concept of white superiority so associated with the South was by no means restricted to the South—it was a part of the nineteenth-century assumptions of most Americans. In dis-

tant Oregon, far removed from the struggle over slavery, there
was a provision in the Bill of Rights in its constitution of 1857
which declared:

No free negro or mulatto, not residing in this State at the time of
the adoption of this Constitution, shall come, reside or be within
this State, or hold any real estate, or make any contracts, or maintain any suit therein; and the Legislative Assembly shall provide by
penal laws for the removal by public officers of all such negroes
and mulattoes, and for their effectual exclusion from the State, and
for the punishment of persons who shall bring them into the State,
or employ or harbor them.[30]

Although the Civil War emphatically settled the issue of
slavery, and established this settlement in the Thirteenth
Amendment, it by no means basically altered the generally
accepted white supremacy settlement of the race question.
Outside the South, at the time of the Civil War, patterns of
discrimination followed wherever free Negroes settled; outside
New England the suffrage in the North and West was restricted to whites. Indeed, it may be questioned whether the
Fourteenth and Fifteenth Amendments would have been sponsored in the North following the Civil War had not well over
90 per cent of the Negro population lived in the former Confederate States. Certainly, subsequent efforts in the nineteenth
century to carry out the provisions of these amendments
aroused little sustained Northern enthusiasm for them. "At the
beginning of the twentieth century," Rayford W. Logan has
observed, "what is now called second-class citizenship for
Negroes was accepted by presidents, the Supreme Court, Congress, organized labor, the General Federation of Women's
Clubs—indeed by the vast majority of Americans, North and
South, and by the 'leader' of the Negro race." [31]

The Fourteenth Amendment, ratified in 1868, declared in its
most crucial section that:

All persons born or naturalized in the United States, and subject
to the jurisdiction thereof, are citizens of the United States and
of the State wherein they reside. No State shall make or enforce
any law which shall abridge the privileges or immunities of citizens

of the United States; nor shall any State deprive any person of life, liberty, or property, without due process of law; nor deny to any person within its jurisdiction the equal protection of the laws.

If, as Senator Jacob Howard of Michigan argued in the debate over the language of the amendment, it was intended to "destroy all caste and class in the United States," it clearly failed to accomplish its purpose, for a series of Supreme Court interpretations virtually blocked this intended result. For example, in 1875 Congress passed a public accommodations act not dissimilar to that proposed by President Kennedy in 1963. The preamble stated that "we recognize the equality of all men before the law, and hold it is the duty of government in all its dealings with the people to mete out equal and exact justice to all, of whatever nativity, race, color, or persuasion, religious or political." The act provided penalties for those convicted of denying "the full and equal enjoyment of the accommodations, facilities, and privileges of inns, public conveyances on land or water, theaters, and other places of public amusement." In the *Civil Rights Cases* of 1883—there were seven of them, only two of which were from the South—the Supreme Court found that the law was unconstitutional since the Fourteenth Amendment was binding only upon states, not upon individuals (or private establishments or businesses), and Congress lacked the authority to pass general legislation on the subject. Justice Harlan dissented, and in memorable words observed:

I cannot resist the conclusion that the substance and spirit of the recent amendments of the Constitution have been sacrificed by a subtle and ingenious verbal criticism. Constitutional provisions, adopted in the interest of liberty, and for the purpose of securing, through national legislation, if need be, rights inhering in a state of freedom, and belonging to American citizenship, have been so construed as to defeat the ends the people desired to accomplish by changes in the fundamental law. . . . We shall enter upon an era of constitutional law, when the rights of freedom and American citizenship cannot receive from the nation that efficient protection which heretofore was unhesitatingly accorded to slavery and the rights of the master.[32]

The Civil Rights Act of 1875 was the last Congressional civil rights legislation for 82 years.

The Fifteenth Amendment, ratified in 1870, declared that: "The right of citizens of the United States to vote shall not be denied or abridged by the United States or by any state on account of race, color, or previous condition of servitude." It, too, had to run the gauntlet of judicial interpretation. In *United States v. Reese* (1876) it was found that this amendment did not confer a right of suffrage but simply prohibited its denial for the stated reasons. Accordingly, sections of the Enforcement Act of 1870 were found unconstitutional in that they provided penalties for in any way hindering a person in voting. In 1894 Congress repealed the entire statute and passed no further legislation on the subject until 1957.

By the end of the nineteenth century, "Jim Crow" provisions became an accepted part of American constitutional law, and probably of public opinion as well. In *Plessy v. Ferguson* (1896) such a "Jim Crow" law requiring separate railway coaches for whites and Negroes in Louisiana was contended to be incompatible with the Fourteenth Amendment. Justice Henry B. Brown, writing the majority opinion, found no such incompatibility.

The object of the amendment was undoubtedly to enforce the absolute equality of the two races before the law, but in the nature of things it could not have been intended to abolish distinctions based upon color, or to enforce social, as distinguished from political, equality, or a commingling of the two races upon terms unsatisfactory to either. Laws permitting, and even requiring their separation in places where they are liable to be brought into contact do not necessarily imply the inferiority of either race to the other, and have been generally, if not universally, recognized as within the competency of the state legislatures in the exercise of their police power. The most common instance of this is connected with the establishment of separate schools for white and colored children. . . . We cannot say that a law which authorizes or even requires the separation of the two races in public conveyances is unreasonable or more obnoxious to the 14th Amendment than the acts of Congress requiring separate schools for colored children in the District of Columbia, the constitutionality of which does not seem to have been questioned, or the corresponding acts of state legislatures. . . . Legislation is powerless to eradicate racial instincts or to abolish distinctions based upon physical differences, and the attempt to do so can only result in accentuating the difficulties of the present situation. . . . If one race be inferior to the other socially, the Constitution of the United States cannot put them upon the same plane.[33]

Justice Harlan again entered a strong dissent, in the course of which he inquired whether, if it were permissible to segregate train passengers on the basis of race, would it not be equally permissible to segregate them on the basis of religion? Would it not also be reasonable to expect "That astute men of the dominant race, who affect to be disturbed at the possibility that the integrity of the white race may be corrupted, or that its supremacy will be imperiled," by sitting with Negroes in passenger cars, would seek segregation in the jury box? "The thin disguise of 'equal' accommodations for passengers in railroad coaches will not mislead anyone, or atone for the wrong this day done." However, the combination of national indifference to and acceptance of the decision would seem to suggest that it was fundamentally satisfying to the white community at large. An extreme, but probably not too rare, Northern view of the proper relationship between whites and Negroes was expressed by Madison Grant some twenty years after the *Plessy v. Ferguson* decision.

   The native American has always found and finds now in the black men willing followers who ask only to obey and to further the ideals and wishes of the master race, without trying to inject into the body politic their own views, whether racial, religious or social. Negroes are never socialists or labor unionists and as long as the dominant imposes its will on the servient and as long as they remain in the same relation to the whites as in the past, the Negroes will be a valuable element in the community but once raised to social equality their influence will be destructive to themselves and to the whites.[34]

It seems evident in retrospect that, as long as 90 per cent of the Negro population remained in the South, a fundamental change in the accepted values of white supremacy could not occur. In the South the association of Negroes with slavery instilled a relationship between the races that could not be easily overcome; outside the South there were too few Negroes to present an effective political demand to a fundamentally indifferent white community. The North came to regard the race question as peculiarly a Southern problem as slavery had been before it. Therefore, it was not a national issue but a sectional one. *The Nation*, for example, could write off the issue in 1886 with the statement that "the nation no longer has a negro problem to settle." [35] In addition, some circles believed that in time the race problem would disappear. In 1810, in the first census after the ending of the foreign slave trade, the Negro population represented 19 per cent of all Americans. In every census thereafter throughout the nineteenth century this percentage declined. By 1930 the percentage of Negroes in the population had dropped to its lowest point, 9.7 (in 1960 it was 10). Thus, for decades following the Civil War it was not unreasonable to assume that the race question was of declining importance and essentially geographically restricted to the South. Such a view might have continued to be the accepted perspective for an even longer period of time had there not been the vast shift in Negro population, beginning about the time of the First World War, which stimulated a shift in social values. This population shift was further accelerated by the Second World War. Then, however, the attendant shift in social values gained impetus from the rise of the political significance of Africa in world politics, and the consequent American effort to win allies among the emerging nations.

*

Issues of race, status, and income have been historically intertwined. This interrelationship has been present whenever Caucasians have encountered any number of nonwhites in what was traditionally looked upon in the nineteenth century as "the white man's country." The entrance of Asians into California furnishes many interesting parallels to the biracialism found in the South.

"Forty years ago the California race problem was essentially a Chinese problem," Governor William D. Stephens wrote in 1920. "At that time our Japanese population was negligible. The Chinese immigrants, however, were arriving in such numbers that the people of the entire Pacific slope became alarmed at a threatened inundation of our white civilization by this Oriental influx." [36] This wave of immigration had in the space of thirty years brought some 75,000 Chinese into California, which then (1880) had a total population of approximately 865,000.[37] The same period had seen the addition of some seven million white immigrants into the nation at large.

The Chinese first started coming into California shortly after the Gold Rush of 1849. Their increased immigration in the next decade was greatly facilitated by the use of a legal device which was euphemistically called contract labor. It was so similar to slave labor that it alarmed humanitarians generally. Under the contract labor system the contractor would gather up shiploads of Chinese coolies who had contracted to serve him for a term of years as laborers in return for four or five dollars a month plus passage. Upon completion of the passage from China, the contractor would sell his contract to the highest bidder, depositing his cargo of coolies in some foreign port while he rounded up a new shipload in China. There were informal, if violent, means of enforcing the terms of the contract committing the workers to the required years of servitude. The lurid tales of the mass misery and suffocation of this human cargo in the holds of ships engaged in the China trade are nineteenth-century companion pieces to those related earlier to the African slave trade.

It was natural, therefore, that after the Civil War humanitarian forces would join with the fledgling National Labor Union to seek an end to the coolie trade and the contract labor system. Yet, as with the previous case of the African slave

trade, questions of race and status became joined with questions of economics. The issue of the inhumanity of the contract
system to the Chinese became quite lost in the discussion of
the depressed wages resulting from coolie competition and the
prospects of racial conflict resulting from an increasing Chinese
immigration to the Coast. Early Congressional legislation
curbed but did not cut off the entrance of Chinese labor; it
was, therefore, followed, under the skillful leadership of Samuel Gompers of the A.F. of L., by the Chinese Exclusion Act
of 1882, and the 1885 prohibition on the importation of contract labor. "No more vicious racist ideas were ever expressed
than those spewed out by Samuel Gompers in the A.F. of L.
campaign against the Chinese," Oscar Handlin has remarked.[38]
In an era not noted for its solicitude for labor it was nevertheless
possible to pass national legislation favorable to labor when the
issue was put in terms of race.

Typically, the discussion of race in the Chinese Exclusion
Act hearings rejected the concept of racial equality and assumed the domination of one race by another. "To any one
reading the testimony which we lay before the two houses,"
one Congressional commission reported, "it will become painfully evident that the Pacific coast must in time become either
American or Mongolian." [39] Always lying beneath the economic issue of the desirability or undesirability of cheap immigrant labor in California was the racial issue, ready to come
to the surface. After studying the testimony in the hearings on
Chinese immigration, a former minister to China reported
(1881):

I know of no people who have seemed to me to have so many
prejudices of race as ourselves. Whether it is due to our long
contests with tribes of savages, the natives of the vast territory
which we have occupied; or to the institution of slavery which took
upon itself among us, the very worst features which slavery has
ever exhibited; whether it is a pride of stock stimulated by our
successful conquests over the many difficulties attending the settlement of a new, and in some respects, an inhospitable region; or
whether all these have combined to produce the result, it would

seem that a Negro, in times now passing by as we may hope, or a Chinaman still, meets with a less ready reception from us than in any of the European nations. . . . And all the while we cry out, with what to Heaven must appear the grossest delusion and hypocrisy, that these other races resist our influence—that they will not assimilate. We hold them all at arms length and then throttle them because they will not approach nearer to us. This is our boasted liberality and generosity.[40]

*

The attitude of white superiority, which had been present for decades in the American culture, was to be further refined by some in the 1880's into Anglo-Saxon superiority. Josiah Strong, for example, wrote: "There can be no reasonable doubt that North America is to be the great home of the Anglo-Saxon, the principal seat of his power, the center of his life and influence." The new theory of races, appearing under the rubric of social Darwinism, was evident as Strong talked of *the final competition of races, for which the Anglo-Saxon is being schooled.* "If I read not amiss," he observed in an invitation to imperialism, "this powerful race will move down upon Mexico, down upon Central and South America, out upon the islands of the sea, over upon Africa and beyond. And can any one doubt that the results of this competition of races will be the 'survival of the fittest'." [41]

By the turn of the century, however, American racists were questioning the application of the survival-of-the-fittest doctrine in the context of immigration policy. In 1916 Madison Grant wrote *The Passing of the Great Race,* which by 1921 had gone into its fourth edition, with French and German translations. Grant, in fact, credits the book with helping to bring on the national origins system of restrictive immigration in 1921. Boasting of Nordic superiority, he lamented the passing of the great race through what he called the "survival of the unfit," brought about, he maintained, by ameliorative legislation and our generous immigration policy.

By the end of the First World War, innumerable pressures

were building up to restrict immigration further along racial lines. In California, in 1920, out of a total population of nearly three and a half million the Japanese inhabitants numbered approximately 88,000. (The Chinese population in California had by then dropped to about 33,000). "It is apparent," wrote Governor Stephens of California, "without much more effective restrictions that in a very short time, historically speaking, the Japanese population within our midst will represent a considerable portion of our entire population. . . ." Under a 1913 statute, California had forbidden the ownership of agricultural land to Japanese and had restricted their holdings to three-year leases. Now an exclusion act, similar to the Chinese Exclusion Act, was sought. The "mistake of Hawaii must not, and California is determined shall not, be repeated here," the Governor wrote. "We assume no arrogant superiority of race or culture over them [Japanese]." The problem "has no origin in narrow race prejudice or rancor or hostility," he declared as he appealed for the enactment of an initiative measure which would prohibit even the leasing of land by Japanese. "But that our white race will readily intermix with the yellow strains of Asia, and that out of this interrelationship shall be born a new composite human being is manifestly impossible. . . . It may be an exquisite refinement, but we cannot feel contented at our children imbibing their first rudiments of education from the lips of the public school teacher in classrooms crowded with other children of a different race. . . . Unless the race ideals and standards are preserved here at the national gateway the condition that will follow must soon affect the rest of the continent." [42]

In the East a similar pressure for restrictive immigration legislation had been building up for many years, as the source of supply of immigrants moved further into Eastern Europe and Russia. In 1880 there were as many foreign-born whites living in the United States as Negroes (13 per cent). From 1890 to 1910 slightly more than 14 per cent of our population consisted of foreign-born whites. In the large cities, as well as in the Populist farm belt, anti-Semitism was on the rise, bring-

ing additional pressure to curtail immigration. The race argument had turned from white supremacy to Anglo-Saxon or
Nordic superiority. The changing composition of America
fomented a conflict in social values which eventually affected
immigration policy. The social origin of social values may be
seen in the opposing views of two late nineteenth-century
poets. Emma Lazarus, a New York Jew, saw the great influx
of immigrants and wrote: "Give me your tired, your poor,
your huddled masses yearning to breathe free. . . ." Thomas
Bailey Aldrich, New Hampshire-born editor of the *Atlantic
Monthly*, saw this same influx and expressed his alarm (in
"Unguarded Gates") at the "Accents of menace alien to our
air, Voices that once the Tower of Babel knew. . . . "[43] It
was the Aldrich view which ultimately triumphed in our immigration laws. After 1921, in statutes culminating in the National
Origins Act of 1929 (and continued in the McCarran-Walter
Immigration Act of 1952), immigration from outside the Western hemisphere was restricted essentially to Europeans, and
those in proportion to the national origins of our population
in 1920. For all practical purposes, the further development of
racial diversity would have to come about by natural increase
in the domestic population.

❋

It is evident in the light of the above that the effort to realize
the equalitarian ideals of the Declaration of Independence and
the constitutional requirements of the Fourteenth Amendment
has been fraught with monumental difficulties. For, in effect,
the Fourteenth Amendment has called upon Americans to deal
equally with those whom the national immigration laws stig-
matize as unequals. In some respects the national struggle for
racial equality today is comparable to the struggle for religious
equality in colonial Massachusetts at the time when the Puritans were still prohibiting the entry of Quakers. Yet, ironically, the National Origins Act has probably been conducive
thus far to promoting racial equality in America by curbing

the entry of cheap white immigrant labor in the Northern cities.

It was not until the Second World War that Americans awoke from the appalling apathy that had characterized public opinion on racial discrimination in the past. Hitler's anti-Semitism, in part echoed by American fascist groups in the late 1930's, together with the atrocities committed by the Nazis in the name of Nordic superiority, caused a revulsion against race theory in this country that led in turn to a re-examination of public policy as well as private sentiment. No country which had seen the lynching of 119 Negroes (according to the Tuskegee Institute records) during the decade of the thirties could fight a war against blatant racism with entirely clean hands.

As the war with the Nazis brought home to many Americans the evils of racism, so the global struggle for power after the war had its effect on our public policy. With the fractionalization of old colonial empires into new national states, it was politically desirable to win over native governments to the United States. In many areas of the world, since white was the color of colonialism, the treatment of nonwhite minorities took on international importance. Now, for the first time in our history, it became of concern to Americans how Africans felt about the American treatment of Negroes. This factor was noted in the U.S. Commission on Civil Rights *Report* of 1961: "The emergence of new nonwhite nations in Africa and Asia does not make an inequity any more unjust. It may, however, make remedial action more urgent." [44] In the domestic struggle for equal rights the rise of the nonwhite nations introduced a new factor into American politics, favorable to the cause of racial equality.

In 1909 the National Association for the Advancement of Colored People was founded to promote the cause of equal rights for Negroes. The following year the Urban League was established to forward equal employment, housing, and welfare services for Negroes. In 1915 the venerable Booker T. Washington died, and with his death passed an era of passivity and general acceptance of second-class citizenship for Negroes.

66 EQUALITY IN AMERICA

New voices were now heard: W. E. B. DuBois proclaiming Pan-Africanism; Father Divine with his "Peace Movement," which began in 1915; Noble Drew Ali, who founded his first Moorish-American Science Temple in 1913; Marcus Garvey who established a Harlem branch of the Universal Negro Improvement Association in 1917.

These Negro movements reflected not only a rising sense of awareness on the part of Negroes, but also, with the First World War, the population shift of Negroes into the Northern cities. This population movement continued during the 1920's as agriculture, geared to an uncontrolled war production of crops, felt the first touches of the depression which would later hit the cities. The depression in agriculture, together with the greater economic opportunities for unskilled labor to be had in the industrialized areas, now that the immigration of white unskilled labor was restricted, spurred on the Negro exodus from the Southern farms. The quota system of immigration restriction deprived the urban industrialized areas of the supply of cheap unskilled labor that Negro workers were willing and able to provide. "Thereafter," Oscar Handlin noted in his New York metropolitan region study, "the need for the type of labor the immigrants had supplied would have to be met from sources not covered by the immigration law—from within the United States and its territorial possessions." [45] A considerable economic incentive was thereby offered to Negroes (and Puerto Ricans) to migrate to New York and other Northern cities. Ironically, the implicit racism behind the immigration laws fostered the entry of Negroes into cities which had generally barred all immigrants except those from England, Ireland, and northwestern Europe. Negroes have thus fully participated in the urban movement which has so characterized twentieth-century America. It was, of course, some recognition of the changing status of Negroes that led white supremacists in 1915 to organize the modern Ku Klux Klan, which reached its peak of activities and influence in the twenties.

This population shift of Negroes, which continues today, has been of inestimable importance in the movement toward equal rights. It has on the one hand diminished the concentration of Negroes in the South, where the attitudes of whites have been most intransigent and the subservience of Negroes most conditioned, and on the other it has brought Negroes into political significance in the North, even as it has awakened whites there to the existence of a problem many had heretofore preferred to overlook. In 1896, when the Supreme Court decided *Plessy v. Ferguson*, over 90 per cent of the nation's Negroes lived in the South; in 1954, when the Court rejected the "separate but equal" doctrine by declaring in *Brown v. Board of Education* that "separate education facilities are inherently unequal," nearly half of the Negro population lived outside the South. By 1960 there were more Negroes in New York than in any other state in the Union. Only Louisiana, Georgia, North Carolina, and Texas, of the Southern states, had a larger Negro population than Illinois. California and Pennsylvania each had more Negroes than either South Carolina or Virginia; Michigan and Ohio each had more Negroes than Maryland or Tennessee. The exodus of Negroes from the South left an overwhelming white majority in most Southern states by 1960; only in Mississippi, with its white majority of 58 per cent, was there anything near an approximation of numerical equality in racial composition. No longer could it be said, if indeed it ever could have been, that race relations in the United States were a sectional problem; clearly they were a national, and additionally, an urban problem.

The urbanization of Negroes had reached the point where, in 1960, some 90 per cent of all Northern Negroes lived in urban areas, and this population in turn was increasing rapidly. According to the 1961 *Report* of the U.S. Commission on Civil Rights:

The proportion of Negroes in the population of Chicago, Cleveland, New York, and Philadelphia more than doubled between 1940 and 1960; in Cleveland, Detroit, and Los Angeles it tripled; in San Francisco, it increased more than twelvefold. There is every indication that the minority proportion of most cities' population will continue to increase because of further migration, the relatively higher birth rate among nonwhites, and a continued exodus of whites to the suburbs. If present trends continue, even those cities which now have small Negro populations will have a sizeable proportion within 10 or 20 years.[46]

The changing character of the urban constituency has inevitably been reflected in its choice of political candidates and in their public policies. This political change is most clearly seen in the contrast between urban voting patterns of forty years ago and those of today. In 1920, as James MacGregor Burns has pointed out, Harding carried every borough in New York City for the Republican party, while four years later Coolidge carried the twelve largest cities with a million votes to spare.[47] Today, however, the cities are predominantly Democratic and the Negro vote overwhelmingly so. The *Newsweek* poll of July 1963, conducted by Louis Harris, reported that 86 per cent of non-Southern Negroes were for Kennedy in 1960, while approximately the same percentage favored his re-election in 1964.[48] The vote of Northern urban Negroes is not a political factor that is likely to be overlooked in Presidential elections. The revolution in the rights of Negroes can be viewed as a part, albeit a vital one, of a larger political change that has been produced by the urbanization—with its complex interdependencies—of American life.

The nature of our political system is such that it has often been the Presidential branch of the government, nationally elected, which has first felt the political imperatives of a social change in the making. The President's role, in turn, facilitates his assumption of leadership in movements of social change. It was therefore not surprising that the combination of domestic and international politics in the late 1930's—the Negro shift in population at home and Nazi racism and war abroad— should have caused the executive branch of government under President Roosevelt to take cognizance of certain new imperatives.

Civil rights in World War II, in fact, became a correlative issue to national defense under the leadership of the Commander in Chief. In 1939, the year in which the Second World

War began, the Civil Rights Section was created in the Department of Justice to prosecute violators of the limited Civil Rights Act of Reconstruction days. In 1941, the year of Pearl Harbor, President Roosevelt established the Fair Employment Practices Committee by executive order. In 1943 another executive order created the practice of "no discrimination" clauses in defense contracts, and after the war ended still another executive order, this one issued by President Truman in 1946, established the President's Committee on Civil Rights, whose report in 1947 brought to many people an awareness of the extent of racial discrimination as well as recommendations on how to remove it. "The protection of civil rights is a national problem which affects everyone," the committee reported. "We need to guarantee the same rights to every person regardless of who he is, where he lives, or what his racial, religious, or national origins are." [49] In 1948, again by executive order, President Truman prohibited racial segregation in the armed forces.

During these same troubled years Congress acted on civil rights only to the extent that in 1942 it passed the Soldiers' Vote Act which removed the poll tax as a prerequisite for voting for members of the armed forces during the war. In all, it might be said that the first phase of the modern equal rights movement, the phase in which the landmarks were the wartime executive orders, looked less like a rights movement than a movement to achieve high productivity and high morale in national defense.

The Second World War and its defense-related activities, which placed such heavy demands upon Negro manpower, accelerated the pace of the Negroes' change of status. Defense industries brought better jobs, better pay, some protection against discrimination in employment, better prospects for the education of children, and a mobility which threatened the parochialism implicit in segregation. In all, the defense industries, together with the draft, brought a new degree of sophistication into the movement toward equality, a new militancy into Negro leadership, a new standard of expectations into the rank-and-file membership, and a new awareness among many whites of the nature of the issue. It was unlikely that when they came of age Negro babies of the Second World War era would be satisfied with less than at least legal equality in the community at large, nor was it likely that the changing conscience of many white Americans would further tolerate the discrimination that had been practiced in the past. A public policy of racial equality which had once been a necessity of national defense thus became, a generation later in the 1960's, a necessity of public peace.

Behind the racial tensions of the 1960's lay a Negro generation acutely aware of extreme frustration. Unskilled Negro workers, the first to be fired from jobs during recessions, the last to be hired during prosperity, lived on the uncertain fringes of the white community, despite all their rising expectations engendered by the war. The imperatives of high morale and full employment which had given some promise of equal rights in time of war seemed no longer essential to many whites in time of peace. In 1945 when the war ended, Congress ceased appropriating funds to sustain the Fair Employment Practices Committee, effectively ending the life of that limited experiment while giving the nation some foretaste of the Congressional response to the movement for equal rights. Nor was indeed any positive legislation in the field of race relations expected of the Congress, which had not passed any significant civil rights legislation since 1875, and whose seventy years of silence on the subject gave little promise for the future.

Essentially the movement for equal rights for Negroes encompassed six broad areas of concern, in no way different from those of other Americans: equality in the opportunities for employment, private housing, public accommodations, schooling, politics, and the administration of justice. In each of these areas, as America entered the Second World War, a curtain was drawn around the Negro. There were no fair employment laws prohibiting discrimination on the grounds of race (by 1961 twenty-one states had such laws), nor was there any prohibition against racial discrimination in defense industries.[50]

Public housing projects generally provided segregated housing for Negroes (in 1962 President Kennedy banned segregation in federal public housing projects by executive order); while private housing was limited in availability due to the common practice of racial restrictive covenants. Discrimination on grounds of race was common in schools and colleges throughout the country, and in seventeen states, as well as in the District of Columbia, segregated schooling was required by law. Segregated accommodations in trains, buses, and public facilities were also common practices, as well as, in many states, requirements of the law.

Negroes were thus restricted both by custom and law to second-class citizenship. But the laws which restricted Negroes could not in turn be altered by Negroes, for in the South they were effectively barred from political participation. At the end of the 1930's, eight Southern states restricted Negro voting through use of the poll tax (in 1963, five states retained the poll tax as a prerequisite for voting, but thirty-two states had ratified an anti-poll tax amendment proposed by Congress in 1962), while most of the one-party Southern states restricted Negro voting by use of the white primary.

The inability of Negroes to exert political influence in Southern politics, together with the refusal of Congress to legislate in the area of civil rights, caused Negroes to turn to the federal courts for relief. In the absence of reform legislation, and given the conservative record of judicial decisions, the prospect was not promising. In the 1920's the Supreme Court had struck down white primaries in Texas as contrary to the Fourteenth Amendment, but in the more turbulent thirties the Court had permitted a wide loophole in *Grovey v. Townsend* (1935), which was the only major case before it on that subject in that decade. This was followed by *Breedlove v. Suttles* (1937), which in effect upheld the constitutionality of the poll tax as a prerequisite for voting. The leading case on public facilities was still the ancient *Plessy v. Ferguson* (1896), with its implied "separate but equal" doctrine, while the guiding case on racial restrictive covenants in housing was *Corrigan v. Buckley*

(1926), in which they had been upheld as private agreements. In all of the 1930's the only case before the Supreme Court which gave any promise of the revolution in rights to come with the war was *Missouri ex. rel. Gaines v. Canada* (1938), in which it was held that Missouri, which had no separate Negro law school, could not satisfy the equal protection clause of the Fourteenth Amendment by subsidizing the tuition of a Negro student to attend a law school outside the state rather than admit him to the law school of the University of Missouri.

With the war came also a general change of personnel on the Supreme Court, the Roosevelt appointees of the latter days of the New Deal. This court, taking a more expansive view of national power than had its immediate predecessor, commenced an assault upon the traditional racially restrictive rulings of the past, an assault which gained in momentum over the years. In 1941, segregation in Pullman cars fell before the new view of the commerce power, and, before the decade of the forties ended, most forms of segregation in interstate transportation had been prohibited. In 1944, the decision in *Smith v. Allwright* finally outlawed the white primary, asserting that:

It may now be taken as a postulate that the right to vote in such a primary for the nomination of candidates without discrimination by the State, like the right to vote in a general election, is a right secured by the Constitution. By the terms of the Fifteenth Amendment that right may not be abridged by any State on account of race. Under our Constitution the great privilege of the ballot may not be denied a man by the State because of his color.

This overruled *Grovey v. Townsend*, decided by a unanimous Court only nine years earlier, when some of the major acts of the New Deal were being found null and void. Dissenting was Justice Roberts, the last remaining judge who had heard the earlier case. "It is regrettable that in an era marked by doubt and confusion," he wrote, "an era whose greatest need is steadfastness of thought and purpose, this court, which has been looked to as exhibiting consistency in adjudication, and a steadiness which would hold the balance even in the face of temporary ebbs and flows of opinion, should now itself become the breeder of fresh doubt and confusion in the public mind as to the stability of our institutions." [51] Four years later, in *Shelley v. Kraemer* (1948), the enforceability of racially restrictive covenants in state courts fell before the equal protection clause of the Fourteenth Amendment. "It cannot be doubted that among the civil rights intended to be protected from discriminatory state action by the Fourteenth Amendment are the rights to acquire, enjoy, own and dispose of property," the court observed.[52] Clearly the social revolution in the status of Negroes was given both recognition and encouragement in the rulings of the Supreme Court.

Although many of the traditional forms of legal restrictions were toppling—in interstate transportation, in primary elections, in housing, and in many states in employment, for many Negroes the progress still was painfully slow. The big bottleneck—equal educational opportunity—remained. Without equal opportunity for public education most Negroes remained ill-equipped to compete with their better-educated white contemporaries. They would have to take unskilled jobs at poorer pay with less certainty of secure employment prospects; this meant low-cost housing in slums or marginal slum areas; it meant a greater health problem for those with least ability to pay for medical expenses; and, finally, it meant their children would be going to inferior and ill-equipped schools where intellectual motivation was low and drop-outs were high, so that the vicious circle would be repeated in the next generation. Even though all other forms of racial discrimination were removed, inferior education for Negroes would tend to perpetuate a semi-caste system of racial relationships.

In still another respect, equal educational opportunity was a necessity for racial equality, because traditionally the public schools have broken down class barriers. A nondiscriminatory policy of employment for adults could hardly be based upon a system of segregated schooling for children. With integrated schooling so fundamentally the root of the matter for whites as well as Negroes, the National Association for the Advancement of Colored People sought to have the old "separate but equal" doctrine overturned. Early in 1950 the time seemed propitious for such an assault on the old ruling, and a case was brought in the federal court in Charleston, South Carolina, on behalf of some sixty-seven Negro children and parents. A year later, a federal court upheld the "separate but equal" doctrine but by a 2–1 vote, and the decision was appealed to the Supreme Court. In the meantime, in 1950, in *Sweatt v. Painter* and *McLaurin v. Oklahoma State Regents* the Supreme Court had already edged toward cognizance of the issue that would soon come before it, by observing in the majority opinion of the former case:

To what extent does the Equal Protection Clause of the Fourteenth Amendment limit the power of a state to distinguish between students of different races in professional and graduate education in a state university? Broader issues have been urged for our consideration, but we adhere to the principle of deciding constitutional questions only in the context of the particular case before the Court. We have frequently reiterated that this Court will decide constitutional questions only when necessary to the disposition of the case at hand, and that such decisions will be drawn as narrowly as possible. Because of this traditional reluctance to extend constitutional interpretations to situations or facts which are not before the Court, much of the excellent research and detailed argument presented in these cases is unnecessary to their disposition.[53]

In the cases at hand the court held that to refuse a qualified Negro admission to the University of Texas law school on the grounds that the state provided a separate law school for Negroes was a violation of the equal protection clause of the Fourteenth Amendment; and the equal protection clause was also violated in Oklahoma when that state segregated in campus facilities a Negro graduate student previously admitted. So by 1950 the court had found that the Fourteenth Amendment gave equal protection to otherwise qualified Negro students seeking advanced degrees at previously segregated white institutions of learning.

The question was still open, however, whether racial segregation was permissible at lesser levels of education. This would be settled shortly by the case involving the sixty-seven Negro children and parents which had started in Charleston in 1950 and was still on its historic path. The Supreme Court returned the case to the lower court for further action; but the further action only produced a second appeal to the Supreme Court. Evidently the issue could no longer be evaded, for the South Carolina case was joined with four others of a similar nature in the fall of 1952 under the title *Brown v. Board of Education*. The title was derived from the companion case of Oliver Brown, who was suing the Board of Education of Topeka, Kansas, to gain admittance for his eight-year-old daughter to the public school nearest to his home rather than to the more distant Negro school. Not since the Dred Scott case of nearly a century before had any Supreme Court case held such momentous import for the future of American Negroes. It was estimated that the education of some three million Negroes in segregated schools alone could be affected by the decision; in the segregated states alone there were more than twice as many Negroes as there were in the entire United States at the time of the Dred Scott decision (1857).

Because of the tremendous significance of the cases both sides carefully picked their attorneys: Thurgood Marshall (later a federal judge) of the NAACP led the staff for the plantiffs; John W. Davis, the Democratic Party's candidate for President in 1924, led the attorneys for the defense. Although the cases were argued in the fall of 1952 it was not until June 1953 that an announcement came from the Supreme Court. The cases were to be reargued in October when counsels were requested to answer certain basic questions involving the intentions of the framers of the Fourteenth Amendment as well as the powers of the judiciary to remove segregated schooling under it. After reargument in October, at which time Attorney General Herbert Brownell also appeared to attack the constitutionality of segregated public schooling, the Supreme Court again delayed its decision. It was not until May 17, 1954, four years plus one day from the time the sixty-seven Negroes had filed suit in Charleston, South Carolina, that the Court took the momentous step of striking down segregation in the public schools with a unanimous decision. Chief Justice Earl Warren, who had actually come to the Supreme Court after the first appearance of the case from Charleston, wrote the opinion:

In each of the cases, minors of the Negro race, through their legal representatives, seek the aid of the courts in obtaining admission to the public schools of their community on a nonsegregated basis. In each instance, they had been denied admission to schools attended by white children under laws requiring or permitting segregation according to race. This segregation was alleged to deprive the plaintiffs of the equal protection of the laws under the Fourteenth Amendment. . . .

The plaintiffs contend that segregated public schools are not 'equal' and cannot be made 'equal,' and that hence they are deprived of the equal protection of the laws. . . .

In approaching this problem, we cannot turn the clock back to 1868 when the Amendment was adopted, or even to 1896 when *Plessy v. Ferguson* was written. We must consider public education in the light of its full development and its present place in American life throughout the Nation. . . .

Today, education is perhaps the most important function of state and local governments. Compulsory school attendance laws and the great expenditures for education both demonstrate our recognition of the importance of education to our democratic society. It is required in the performance of our most basic public responsibilities, even service in the armed forces. It is the very foundation of good citizenship. Today it is a principal instrument in awakening the child to cultural values, in preparing him for later professional training, and in helping him to adjust normally to his environment. In these days, it is doubtful that any child may reasonably be expected to succeed in life if he is denied the opportunity of an education. Such an opportunity, where the state has undertaken to provide it, is a right which must be made available to all on equal terms.

We come then to the question presented: Does segregation of children in public schools solely on the basis of race, even though the physical facilities and other 'tangible' factors may be equal, deprive the children of the minority group of equal educational opportunities? We believe that it does. . . .

We conclude that in the field of public education the doctrine of 'separate but equal' has no place. Separate educational facilities are inherently unequal. Therefore, we hold that the plaintiffs and others similarly situated for whom the actions have been brought are, by reason of the segregation complained of, deprived of the equal protection of the laws guaranteed by the Fourteenth Amendment.[54]

The Supreme Court, well aware of the far-reaching consequences of its decision, did not follow through with an enforcement order but rescheduled hearings for the fall of 1954 on how the decision in *Brown v. Board of Education* might be carried out. While some school districts moved to integrate their white and Negro students in the fall term, most school boards held back awaiting a further order from the court. In May 1955, five years after the filing of the initial case and near the end of still another school year, the Supreme Court issued its enforcement decision. Again, the opinion was written by Chief Justice Earl Warren. Full responsibility would fall upon the local school boards for implementing the decision, under the surveillance of the courts which initially heard the cases. The courts in turn would be "guided by equitable principles," which might "properly take into account the public interest" in achieving nondiscriminatory schools. "But it should go without saying that the vitality of these constitutional principles cannot be allowed to yield simply because of disagreement with them." The cases were thus remanded to the District Courts "to take such proceedings and enter such orders and decrees consistent with this opinion as are necessary and proper to admit to public schools on a racially nondiscriminatory basis with all deliberate speed the parties to these cases." [55]

With the destruction of the doctrine of "separate but equal" in *Brown v. Board of Education,* a milestone was passed in American constitutional history, yet in its immediate practical significance it marked only a slight step forward. For a massive resistance movement was mounted in several Southern states in which state law and public opinion were marshaled to "inter-pose" the verdict of the Court. In March of 1956 some one hundred Senators and Representatives signed a "Southern Man-ifesto" which brought moral support to those resisting inte-gration, as it declared: "We commend the motives of those states which have declared the intention to resist forced inte-gration by any lawful means. . . ." [56] By 1958 over one hun-dred laws had been enacted in various Southern states, intended to avoid the consequences of the decision.[57] Because of the high cost of litigation to carry a case to the Supreme Court—Senator Javits reported that the average cost was $18,000 "exclusive of counsel's fees"—this put an impossible economic burden on those least able to pay the high costs of legally de-fending their rights. The social and economic pressure upon Negroes was equally severe in still another way. For example, in Clarendon County, South Carolina, when the sixty-seven Negroes initially had sought desegregated schooling in 1950 by bringing their case to the District Court in Charleston, economic reprisals were introduced. Negro parents found work denied to them, harvesting machinery unavailable to them, a refusal by wholesalers to sell to them, and their names placed on a black list so that they could not get credit locally.[58] Clarendon County, indeed, is not scheduled to begin desegrega-tion in the schools until 1965, fifteen years after the original case was filed, long after the children of the original petitioners will have passed school age. Gradualism, to paraphrase William Lloyd Garrison, tends to result in perpetuity in practice.

If the first phase of the movement toward equal rights may be seen as the national defense phase, in which progress was largely achieved through executive orders, the second phase may be seen as one of constitutional change, in which the major instrument has been litigation and the major immediate goals the removal of legal barriers to racial equality. Although this latter phase necessarily continues (as, of course, does the first), its high point was the principle established in *Brown v. Board of Education* which has guided subsequent decisions in a great variety of areas and is likely to do so for some time.

For example, in 1957, in a clearly discriminatory move, the Alabama legislature redefined the boundaries of the city of Tuskegee to remove from the city Tuskegee Institute and all but a few hundred Negro residents. There was specularion before the case settling the question (*Gomillion v. Lightfoot*) was decided by the Supreme Court in 1960 whether the Court would hold this gerrymandering to be a political question outside of its jurisdiction, or a civil rights question and within it. But there was no uncertainty in the mind of the Assistant Solicitor General, Philip Elman, who appeared in the case as *Amicus curiae*, and who surmised correctly that the case would go to the Negro plantiffs. He observed after argument had been completed,

When one tries to guess the outcome of a case, he can't merely analyze the various precedents, or weigh the conflicting arguments, or speculate as to what the justices may be thinking on the basis of the questions they have asked during the argument. You have to consider what the consequences of the alternative rulings might be. The Supreme Court justices are a realistic and sophisticated group of men. When they weigh a constitutional or civil-rights case, they are not engaged—as laymen tend to think—in a mere legalistic scrutiny of precedents. Justices must also take into account the effect their rulings will have on the country's welfare and the values it lives by. And in those terms, in the Tuskegee case, no matter what arguments we've heard or what surprises may have occurred in some of the justices' questions, it's absolutely inconceivable to me that in this present era the court could rule in favor of the respondents and sanction so blatant a racial discrimination. I just can't conceive of it.[59]

Although the Supreme Court with remarkable consistency struck down racially discriminatory barriers in a variety of areas, litigation was slow and costly, while the obstacles were numerous, formidable, and at times ingenious. Executive action authorized by the President and judicial orders emanating from the federal courts were not enough in the face of hostile state legislatures and a silent Congress. Such progress as was made toward desegrated schools and public facilities took place mainly in the border states and in the urban areas. The state legislatures drew their support primarily from rural areas where there was little social mobility and a generally lower level of education. In these areas, memories were long and traditions ran deep. Atlanta, Dallas, or Greensboro might give way to social change, but in the little towns and county seats the old order was looked upon as settled, satisfactory, and permanent.

The House of Representatives, drawing in the main upon rurally oriented districts, was not unsympathetic to the conservatism of racial discrimination and buried reform bills in committees largely presided over by Southern Congressmen. In the Senate the filibuster made it possible for any demurring minority to block civil rights bills should they emerge from committee. The year of the Court enforcement order in *Brown v. Board of Education*, 1955, was the eightieth year in which the United States Congress failed to pass civil rights legislation. Thus the most significant social movement in postwar America proceeded without the sanction or support of the popular branch of government.

A third phase in the equal rights movement therefore developed, featuring direct action: demonstrations, picketing, sit-ins, economic boycotts, and mass arrests. In 1955 the Montgomery bus boycott began in protest over discrimination in seating in public transportation. From it the name of Martin Luther King, Jr., came into national prominence. In that same year the Interstate Commerce Commission prohibited segregation of interstate passengers, while subsequently the courts ordered the cessation of segregation of bus waiting rooms and terminal restaurants. In February, 1960, the first lunch counter sit-ins started in Greensboro, North Carolina, and soon this form of direct action spread throughout Southern cities. The following year the Freedom Riders brought dramatic attention to the continuation of segregation, and their action led to further Interstate Commerce Commission rulings barring segregation in terminal facilities. By the summer of 1963, a century after the Emancipation Proclamation, there were few days without headlines calling attention to some new form of direct action by Negroes to protest discrimination, while the leadership of the NAACP, the Urban League, the Student Nonviolent Coordinating Committee, the Congress of Racial Equality, and the Southern Christian Leadership Conference organized a dramatic demonstration in Washington on August 28 to stimulate Congress into activity.

Direct action, its proponents hoped, would achieve three things. They hoped to achieve the removal of the discriminatory barriers as far as this was possible without legislation. They hoped that through the attendant publicity the apathetic or indifferent white and Negro consciences might be stimulated so that there would be a genuine awareness of the grievances. And they hoped that Congress would be persuaded to pass legislation which would bring genuine sanction and support to the movement toward racial equality. For many of those opposed to equal rights could agree with the assertion of Senator Jacob Javits of New York, a civil rights champion, "that without the backing of Congress and of law enacted by the Congress civil rights cannot be effectively secured in this country, certainly not within the measurable period of time which is afforded to us for that purpose, considering the pressures under which we labor both at home and abroad."[60]

Yet the composition of Congress, as this reflected both conscience and constituency, was such as to give little promise in 1963 that it was prepared to depart significantly from the traditional social pattern of white supremacy. In 1957 Congress created a temporary six-member Civil Rights Commission whose subsequent investigations, reports, and recommendations called racial discrimination to the attention of the nation. The 1957 act further protected the right to vote, but it was intended to work no fundamental social changes. In 1960 Congress again safeguarded this right by providing for federal referees in voter registration disputes and, finally recognizing *Brown v. Board of Education*, made it a crime to interfere with court desegregation orders. Neither the 1957 nor the 1960 acts reached the fundamental discriminations in economic life or in public accommodations. Yet, while the memory of the incidents at Little Rock, Arkansas; Oxford, Mississippi; and Birmingham, Alabama, were still fresh, it was unlikely that pressure for legislative support of equal rights for some nineteen million Negro Americans would diminish. This pressure was recognized by President Kennedy in June 1963, when he made a dramatic appeal to the nation at the peak of the Tuscaloosa crisis for every American to examine his conscience on the question of race:

We are confronted primarily with a moral issue. It is as old as the Scriptures and is as clear as the American Constitution. The heart of the question is whether all Americans are to be afforded equal rights and equal opportunities; whether we . . . treat our fellow Americans as we want to be treated.

If an American, because his skin is dark, cannot eat lunch in a restaurant open to the public; if he cannot send his children to the best public schools available; if he cannot vote for the public officials who represent him; if, in short, he cannot enjoy the full and free life which all of us want, then who among us would be content to have the color of his skin changed and stand in his place?

Who among us would then be content with the counsels of patience and delay? . . . Now the time has come for this nation to fulfill its promise. . . .

A great change is at hand, and our task, our obligation is to make that revolution, that change peaceful and constructive for all.[61]

To this end President Kennedy submitted a draft of a bill to Congress intended to achieve the "elementary right" of Negroes to receive the same services that others get from businesses serving the public, such as hotels, restaurants, stores, and theaters. The bill also contained a provision to permit fuller participation by the government in school desegregation lawsuits. It was clear that legislation was needed to expedite progress toward equal rights and not alone for its coercive effect; for there were evidently many businessmen who felt that they needed the support of law to undertake the nondiscriminatory practices which they believed right but hesitated to engage in as long as their competitors did not.

In 1964 a decade will have passed since the historic decision of *Brown v. Board of Education.* There is now at least token integration at the higher education level in every state, yet little more than token integration below this level in most of the formerly segregated states. In 1961 it was estimated that in six states, Alabama, Mississippi, Louisiana, South Carolina, Georgia, and Florida, there were 1,600,000 school-age Negroes, less than 1,000 of them in integrated schools. At the end of the school term of 1963 there were no integrated primary or secondary schools in South Carolina, Alabama, and Mississippi. In these three states, desegregation would undoubtedly move slowly because they (along with Arkansas) were the poorest states in the nation in per capita income. Yet Alabama, South Carolina, and Mississippi had the highest proportion of Negroes in their population of any state—31 per cent, 35 per cent, and 42 per cent, respectively. Mississippi had a shockingly low per capita income in 1961 of $1,233, which was less than half of the per capita income, for instance, of the now integrated states Maryland ($2,478) and Delaware ($3,026).

A vicious cycle tends to develop in which poverty makes inadequate schooling inevitable; poor schooling perpetuates prejudice and ignorance, which in turn perpetuate poverty. The bare struggle for existence at the lowest per capita income level in the Deep South, where in about 137 counties Negroes are in the majority, hardly creates the conducive atmosphere in which old patterns of thought and social custom are likely to be put aside in the near future. Yet throughout the South social attitudes were clearly changing, as reflected in public opinion polls. A Gallup poll reported that in 1957 in the South only 45 per cent thought that desegregation was inevitable, while in 1961 some 76 per cent held this view.[62] As industrialization and urbanization proceed in the South (Mississippi is still about 90 per cent rural), income levels may be expected to rise, and with them levels of education.

The importance of education, which has so successfully proven to be a solvent for religious antipathies, is becoming more evident in the area of racial conflict. Once again the role of the Supreme Court in recent years as the national moral censor cannot be underestimated. It is not alone the legal effect of its views in gradually achieving integrated schools and other publicly sponsored social institutions which has been significant, but the equalitarian social values which have guided these decisions and brought an awakened public consciousness to bear upon the problems. Education, broadly considered, serves not only to transmit traditional values but occasionally to transcend them. Recent public opinion surveys have repeatedly shown that racial prejudice is a function of ignorance. "The higher one's education," one social scientist has written, "the more likely one is to believe in democratic values and support democratic practices. All the relevant studies indicate that education is more significant than either income or occupation." [63] These findings are further supported by recent research on the racial attitudes of white Southerners. The most poorly educated whites are the strictest segregationists; the best educated whites are the least segregationist. The higher the level of education the lower the level of racial intolerance.[64] As the national level of education continues to rise, as it has rapidly done since the Second World War, prospects for the amicable and equitable accommodation of racial diversity brighten.

The passage from racial exclusiveness to racial diversity, like the passage from religious exclusiveness to religious diversity, has been historically accompanied by a democratic change in the social basis of politics. As was the case with religious diversity, toleration marks the first step toward equal acceptance. Yet toleration, whether in religious or racial matters, implies a superiority and can therefore never provide a satisfactory, equitable solution to the problems of a heterogeneous and pluralistic society. It may be expected then that "white supremacy," like the semi-official Protestantism of early America, will lose its appeal as a social value as a new equalization of opportunity is more and more realized. Equality thus emerges again as the second-best alternative to that of claimed superiority, with race becoming as irrelevant to public power as religion did. Such a solution to the problem of racial diversity will be

a departure from the practices of the past; yet it will be a
realization of the equalitarian principles of the Declaration of
Independence, which in the words of Lincoln "set up a standard maxim for free society, which should be familiar to all,
and revered by all; constantly looked to, constantly labored
for, and even though never perfectly attained, constantly ap-
proximated, and thereby constantly spreading and deepening
its influence and augmenting the happiness and value of life
to all people of all colors everywhere." [65]

NOTES

1. William Byrd, *The History of the Dividing Line*, William K. Boyd
   (ed.), (Raleigh: The North Carolina Historical Commission, 1929),
   pp. 3–4.
2. Samuel G. Drake, *The Book of the Indians* (Boston: Antiquarian
   Institute, 1837), Book II, p. 63.
3. *Ibid.*, Book V, p. 6.
4. *Ibid.*, p. 66.
5. Helen T. Catterall, *Judicial Cases Concerning American Slavery and
   the Negro* (Washington, 1926–37), I, p. 77, in Edgar T. Thompson
   (ed.), *Race Relations and the Race Problem* (Durham: Duke University Press, 1939), p. 125.
6. For Negro-white ratios from 1790 to 1830 see: Alice Dana Adams,
   The Neglected Period of Anti-Slavery in America (Boston: Ginn
   and Company, 1908), pp. 3–7. The Declaration of Independence
   cannot be said to have been applicable in 1776 to Negroes. "The
   historian of today . . . who would contend that the phrase 'all men'
   was understood by the members of the Continental Congress to
   include Negro slaves has a fragile foundation on which to build."
   Philip F. Detweiler, "Congressional Debate on Slavery and the Declaration of Independence, 1819–1821," *The American Historical
   Review*, 63 (April 1958) 3, pp. 599–600.
7. William Sumner Jenkins, *Pro-Slavery Thought in the Old South*
   (Chapel Hill: The University of North Carolina Press, 1935), p. 29.
8. *Ibid.*, and the references to W. E. B. DuBois, *The Suppression of
   the African Slave Trade to the United States of America, 1638–1870*
   (1896) cited therein. Also see: Kenneth M. Stampp, *The Peculiar
   Institution* (New York: Alfred A. Knopf, Inc., 1956).
9. *Niles' Weekly Register*, Vol. 11, Dec. 14, 1816, p. 260; Dec. 2, 1816,
   p. 275; Dec. 28, 1816, p. 296; Jan. 25, 1817, p. 355.

10. Gunnar Myrdal, *An American Dilemma* (New York: Harper and Brothers, Publishers, 1941), p. 805.

11. Detweiler, *op. cit.*, p. 109.

12. Philip S. Foner, ed., *Basic Writings of Thomas Jefferson* (New York: Wiley Book Co., 1944), pp. 439–40.

13. Jenkins, *op. cit.*, p. 243.

14. John G. Nicolay and John Hay (eds.), *Complete Works of Abraham Lincoln* (Lincoln Memorial Library, 1894), Vol. II, p. 206.

15. Juan Comas, " 'Scientific' Racism Again?" *Current Anthropology*, Oct. 1961, p. 303.

16. William Stanton, *The Leopard's Spots* (Chicago: The University of Chicago Press, 1960), p. 122.

17. The persistence of racist theory in the twentieth century was not only evident in Nazi ideology but in the need felt after the Second World War for a UNESCO-sponsored "Statement on the Nature of Race and Race Differences" by fourteen noted physical anthropologists and geneticists (June 1951), in which it was declared: "Available scientific knowledge provides no basis for believing that the groups of mankind differ in their innate capacity for intellectual and emotional development." Reprinted in *Current Anthropology*, Oct. 1961, pp. 304–6. A decade later, in November 1961, the American Anthropological Association passed a resolution declaring that it "repudiates statements now appearing that Negroes are . . . inferior to Whites and reaffirms the fact that there is no . . . evidence to justify the exclusion of any race from the rights guaranteed by the Constitution of the United States." Quoted in *Current Anthropology*, June 1962, p. 301.

18. Reverend G. T. Gillespie, "A Christian View on Segregation," an address before the Synod of Mississippi of the Presbyterian Church, Nov. 4, 1954, distributed by the Citizens' Councils, Greenwood, Miss., p. 9.

19. *Ibid.*

20. Jenkins, *op. cit.*, p. 205.

21. *Ibid.*, p. 260.

22. Chancellor Harper, "Slavery in the Light of Social Ethics," in *Cotton Is King*, E. N. Elliott (ed.), (Augusta, Ga.: Pritchard, Abbott and Loomis, 1860), p. 593.

23. Judge Tom P. Brady, "Segregation and the South," an address to the Commonwealth Club of California at San Francisco on Oct. 4, 1957, distributed by the Citizens' Councils, Greenwood, Miss., pp. 4–5.

24. *Ibid.*, p. 6.

25. Chancellor Harper, *op. cit.*, p. 549. This line of argument was also seen a century later in Tom P. Brady's *Black Monday* (distributed by the Citizens' Councils): "The American negro was divorced from

RACE 87

Africa and saved from savagery. In spite of his basic inferiority, he was forced to do that which he would not do for himself. He was compelled to lay aside cannibalism, his barbaric savage customs. A moral standard of values was presented to him, a standard he could never have created for himself and which he does not now appreciate." [Tom P. Brady, *Black Monday* (Winona, Miss.: Association of Citizens' Councils, 1955), p. 11.]

26. Senator James O. Eastland, "We've Reached Era [sic] of Judicial Tyranny," an address before the Statewide Convention of the Association of Citizens' Councils of Mississippi; Jackson, Miss., Dec. 1, 1955, p. 9, distributed by the Citizens' Council of Mississippi.

27. *The Works of John C. Calhoun*, Richard K. Crallé (ed.), (New York: D. Appleton and Co., 1854), Vol. III, p. 180.

28. George Fitzhugh, *Cannibals All* (Richmond, Va.: A. Morris, 1857), pp. 94, 315.

29. Tom P. Brady, "Segregation and the South," *op. cit.*, p. 10.

30. Francis N. Thorpe (ed.), *The Federal and State Constitutions* (Washington: U.S. Government Printing Office, 1909), Vol. V, p. 3000.

31. Rayford W. Logan, *The Negro in American Life and Thought* (New York: The Dial Press, Inc., 1954), pp. ix-x.

32. Logan, *op. cit.*, p. 109.

33. Joseph Tussman, *The Supreme Court on Racial Discrimination* (New York: Oxford University Press, 1963), pp. 68-74.

34. Madison Grant, *The Passing of the Great Race* (New York: Charles Scribner's Sons, 1921), pp. 87-8.

35. *The Nation*, 43 (1886) 26. For a fuller discussion of this see: Alan P. Grimes, *The Political Liberalism of the New York Nation, 1865-1932* (Chapel Hill: University of North Carolina Press, 1953), Chapter I, and Alan P. Grimes, "Negro Suffrage and Nineteenth Century Liberalism: Views of the New York *Nation* During Reconstruction," *The Negro History Bulletin*, Dec. 1950.

36. *California and the Oriental*, Report of State Board of Control of California to Governor Wm. D. Stephens (Sacramento, Cal.: 1920), p. 7.

37. Census Bureau figures of June 1880 cited in George F. Seward, *Chinese Immigration* (New York: Charles Scribner's Sons, 1881), p. 421.

38. Oscar Handlin, *Race and Nationality in American Life* (Boston: Little, Brown and Company, 1957), p. 54.

39. Seward, *op. cit.*, p. 294.

40. *Ibid.*, pp. 248-9.

41. Josiah Strong, *Our Country* (New York: Baker & Taylor Co., 1885), pp. 165, 175.

42. *California and the Oriental, op. cit.*, pp. 8, 10, 11, 15.
43. I am indebted to Samuel E. Morison and Henry S. Commager, *The Growth of the American Republic* (New York: Oxford University Press, 1962), Vol. II, pp. 273–75, for this juxtaposition.
44. *U.S. Commission on Civil Rights Report* (Washington: 1961), Vol. I, p. 2.
45. Oscar Handlin, *The Newcomers* (Cambridge: Harvard University Press, 1959), p. 41.
46. *U.S. Commission on Civil Rights Report, op. cit.*, p. 11, notes omitted.
47. James MacGregor Burns, *The Deadlock of Democracy* (Englewood Cliffs, N.J.: Prentice-Hall, Inc., 1963), p. 151.
48. *Newsweek*, July 29, 1963, p. 29.
49. *To Secure These Rights* (New York: Simon and Schuster, Inc., 1947), p. xi.
50. Jacob K. Javits, *Discrimination—U.S.A.* (New York: Washington Square Press, 1962), p. 83.
51. Tussman, *op. cit.*, pp. 356–61.
52. *Ibid.*, p. 289.
53. *Ibid.*, p. 32.
54. *Bown v. Board of Education*, 347 U.S. 483 (1954), reprinted in *ibid.*, pp. 38–42.
55. *Ibid.*, pp. 45–46.
56. Javits, *op. cit.*, pp. 157–8.
57. *Congressional Record*, Feb. 10, 1958, cited in Javits, *op. cit.*, p. 176.
58. Testimony of Billie S. Fleming before Senate Subcommittee on Constitutional Rights, Apr. 16, 1959, cited in Javits, *op. cit.*, pp. 177–78.
59. Bernard Taper, *Gomillion versus Lightfoot* (New York: McGraw-Hill Book Company, Inc., 1962), pp. 109–10.
60. Javits, *op. cit.*, p. 253.
61. Reprinted in *Newsweek*, June 24, 1963, p. 30.
62. *Newsweek*, June 17, 1963, pp. 23–4.
63. Seymour Martin Lipset, *Political Man* (New York: Doubleday & Company, Inc., 1960), p. 56. Also see: Samuel A. Stouffer, *Communism, Conformity, and Civil Liberties* (New York: Doubleday & Company, Inc., 1955).
64. Donald R. Matthews and James W. Prothro, "Southern Racial Attitudes: Conflict, Awareness, and Political Change," *The Annals of the American Academy of Political and Social Science*, Nov. 1962.
65. John G. Nicolay and John Hay (eds.), *Complete Works of Abraham Lincoln* (Lincoln Memorial Library, 1894), Vol. II, p. 331.

3 THE URBAN MAJORITY

Eₐᵣₗᵧ ɪɴ the spring of 1962, a few weeks before the Supreme
Court ruled in the New York Board of Regents prayer case
(*Engel v. Vitale*), and while the political dust was still rising
from desegregation cases, the Supreme Court announced its
decision in *Baker v. Carr*, a reapportionment case from Tennessee. "We conclude," wrote Mr. Justice Brennan for the
majority, "that the complaint's allegations of a denial of equal
protection present a justicial constitutional cause of action
upon which appellants are entitled to a trial and a decision.
The right asserted is within the reach of judicial protection
under the Fourteenth Amendment." [1] With this terse language
the Supreme Court opened up a whole new field of litigation,
since it offered a judicial remedy for a political discrimination.

The facts of the reapportionment case were not unusual; had
they been, the furor following the decision would not have
been so great. In spite of a state constitutional mandate to reapportion its legislature every ten years, the state of Tennessee
had not done so since 1901. So the Tennessee voters of 1960
were still voting in terms of an allocation of seats for the state
legislature laid out in the Apportionment Act of 1901. Given
the vast shifts in population of the past sixty years, the question raised before the Supreme Court was whether the diminished value of individual votes in densely populated districts
today, as a result of the archaic apportionment, discriminated
against the voters in these districts in such a manner as to deny

them the equal protection of the laws guaranteed by the Four-teenth Amendment. In effect the Court ruled that the case was a justiciable one—as opposed to a political question—and within the province of the mandates of the Fourteenth Amendment. Henceforth, it appeared, a remedy for the failure of state legis-latures to apportion equitably could be found in the courts. Inequitable apportionment, in Justice Douglas's concurring opinion, joined race, color, and sex as an additional "imper-missible standard" of voter discrimination. In Tennessee, 37 per cent of the voters controlled 20 of the 33 state Senate seats, while 40 per cent of the voters held 63 of the 99 seats of the House. "If present representation has a policy at all," wrote Justice Clark, concurring, "it is to maintain the *status quo* of invidious discrimination at any cost."

The decision in *Baker v. Carr* provoked a strong and lengthy dissent from Justice Frankfurter, who rejected the view that unequal apportionment was comparable to voter discrimina-tion based on race, color, religion, or sex. "The Court's author-ity—possessed neither of the purse nor the sword—ultimately rests on sustained public confidence in its moral sanction," he wrote. "Such feeling must be nourished by the Court's com-plete detachment, in fact and in appearance, from political entanglements and by abstention from injecting itself into the clash of political forces in political settlements." The majority decision in *Baker v. Carr*, he declared darkly, "may well impair the Court's position as the ultimate organ of 'the supreme Law of the Land' in that vast range of legal problems, often strongly entangled in popular feeling, on which this Court must pro-nounce." The entanglement of the case with strong political feelings became immediately evident, for within the next four-teen months there were cases pending in 37 of the 50 states challenging the existing system of state legislative apportion-ment for one or both houses of the state legislature.

While this onslaught of litigation was indicative of the pres-sures which lay behind the *Baker v. Carr* case on the one hand, the action of the Council of State Governments was indicative of the forces supporting the *status quo* on the other. In De-cember 1962, the Council of State Governments resolved to press for amendments to the Constitution which would not only nullify the Supreme Court's ruling in this case but would further provide for a "Court of the Union" composed of the Chief Justices of the fifty state supreme courts to serve as the highest court in the land. In addition, the Council proposed an amendment to the amending process itself, so that henceforth two-thirds of the state legislatures might initiate constitutional amendments, bypassing Congress or a national convention. As Charles L. Black, Jr. pointed out in the *Yale Law Journal*, if the proposals of the Council of State Governments were adopted as amendments, a combination of inequitably apportioned state legislatures in the thirty-eight least densely populated states could make possible the rule of a minority of 15 per cent over the remaining 85 per cent of the population.[2] "In the last analysis," Justice Harlan wrote in his dissent in *Baker v. Carr,* "what lies at the core of this controversy is a difference of opinion as to the function of representative government."

Behind the whole issue which came to a head in the 1962 case was the vast shift in population over the past sixty years and the consequent question of what this shift portends today in political power and public policy. At the end of the nineteenth century, America was predominantly rural in character and its state legislatures represented predominantly rural constituencies. As the country became urbanized (passing the halfway mark as long ago as 1920), the rural state legislators, reluctant to legislate themselves and the interests they represented out of power, simply failed to keep reapportionments abreast of population shifts. An imbalance, or derangement of representation, thus developed in the state legislative systems, in which the densely populated areas were underrepresented and the sparsely populated areas overrepresented. Faced with the challenge of power from the cities, rural legislators were as reluctant to redistribute districts as feudal landholders had been to redistribute land.

The shift in population which underlies the contemporary problem may be seen succinctly in the dry shorthand of statistics. In 1961 the Bureau of the Budget issued, under the forbidding title of *Standard Metropolitan Statistical Areas*, a list of some 212 population centers. In the last census, which showed our total population to be 179 million, some 112 million were found to be living in these standard metropolitan statistical areas. These areas each included a central city of 50,000 inhabitants or more, as well as surrounding counties where "they are essentially metropolitan in character and are socially and economically integrated with the central city." The areas ranged in population from Meriden, Connecticut (51,850), to the megalopolis of New York (10,694,633), and spread geographically from Portland, Maine, to Honolulu, Hawaii, and from Brownsville, Texas, to Seattle, Washington.

The central cities are familiar to every reader of road maps; and to see them spread across the map is to see the spread of urban-oriented life in America today. For urbanization is not a phenomenon peculiar to the great metropolitan areas such as New York, Los Angeles, Chicago, Philadelphia, and Detroit, with their densely settled populations; it is a common feature in the lives of the 58 million Americans who live in cities with a population of 50,000 and above, and of 54 million other Americans who live immediately adjacent to these cities. Even when we look only at those standard metropolitan statistical areas which have mammoth populations of 900,000 or above, we see that they draw directly into their orbit the residents of twenty states. About twenty-four states have a majority of their population living in metropolitan areas. The states of Washington, Oregon, California, Hawaii, Texas, Nevada, Utah, Arizona, and Colorado have an urban majority in the West, as do Illinois, Ohio, Michigan, Missouri, and Minnesota in the Central region; Maryland, Delaware, Virginia, and Florida in the South, and Massachusetts, Rhode Island, New York, Connecticut, New Jersey, and Pennsylvania in the East. Our urban-oriented existence today is thus in no way a sectional phenomenon; it is found, although in varying degrees, in the North, the South, the Central States, and the West. The problem of providing adequate representation for urban populations in state legislatures is, naturally, as widespread as urbanization itself, though it is felt more acutely in some areas than in others.

In 1955 Gordon E. Baker, in *Rural Versus Urban Political Power*, made a study of urban representation as it then existed in state legislatures. He took selected urban areas in each of the states and computed what percentage of the state population they comprised; he then computed the percentage of seats in each house which this urban area was entitled to under existing apportionments. He found that in Tennessee, for example, the four largest urban counties held 38 per cent of the state's population, yet had only 22 per cent of the seats in the lower house and 20 per cent of the seats in the upper house.[3] Another way of presenting this would be to say that the selected urban area in Tennessee was 16 per cent underrepresented in the house and 18 per cent in the senate. If we list only those states which have a 15 per cent underrepresentation of selected urban areas in the house, we can see how Baker's study points up the extent of this problem.[4]

State	Selected Urban Area	Under-representation House %	Senate %
Connecticut	10 largest cities	−39	0 (approx.)
Florida	9 most urban counties	−37	−36
Vermont	all urban population	−30	0 (approx.)
Delaware	Wilmington urbanized area	−26	−25
Georgia	6 largest urban counties	−23	−25
Maryland	Baltimore and 3 largest urban counties	−23	−36
Nevada	2 largest urban counties	−22	−50
Mississippi	2 largest urban counties	−20	− 4
Kansas	3 largest urban counties	−19	−18
Alabama	3 largest urban counties	−17	−21
Tennessee	4 largest urban counties	−16	−18
Utah	3 largest urban counties	−16	−16
Ohio	8 largest urban counties	−15	0

To this list we may add those states which have less than 15 per cent urban underrepresentation in the house but have 15 per cent or more underrepresentation in the senate. It is

Arizona	2 largest urban counties	0	—55
California	4 largest urban counties	0	—49
Rhode Island	10 largest cities	—10	—43
New Jersey	8 largest urban counties	— 2	—37
Montana	5 largest urban counties	— 5	—28
Oklahoma	2 largest urban counties	—14	—20
Idaho	4 largest urban counties	— 9	—19
New Mexico	largest urban county	—10	—18
Michigan	Wayne County	— 3	—17
Texas	4 largest urban counties	—10	—16
South Carolina	3 largest urban counties	0	—15

evident that most of the states are faced with an urban pressure for reapportionment to give the densely populated areas a greater share of political power, a greater voice in determining public policy.

Behind the reluctance of state legislatures to grant greater political power to urban areas lies more than mere intransigence. Associated with the power are issues, and associated with the issues are attitudes which reflect the opposing pressures mounting in the opposing urban and rural constituencies. The conflict is more than a simple economic contest between the farm and the city; it is rather a complex of attitudes, traditions and cross-pressures which in the politics of today may be symbolized under the labels of conservatism and liberalism. In race, religion, and tradition the rural constituency is essentially homogeneous and its voting behavior conservative. In race, religion, and traditions the urban constituency is pluralistic, heterogeneous, and its voting behavior tends to be liberal. Behind the politics of equality in civil rights and social welfare programs is the dispute over representation in which conservative and liberal constituencies struggle for power in order to control the course of public policy. Since in most states an equitable apportionment of urban areas in accordance with the democratic principle of "one man, one vote" would put urban majorities in both branches of the state legislature, the whole issue of the validity of majority rule has been raised anew in state politics.

*

It was John Locke ("The Great Mr. Locke: America's Philosopher," as the historian Merle Curti once described him) who gave us the classic succinct defense of majority rule. If we could, by a supreme stretch of the imagination, envision a situation in which no man had any authority over any other man, in which there were no traditions of legitimacy for superiority and no compulsions for subordination, if we could wipe the slate clean of power relationships so that we might address ourselves solely to the moral problem of authority, we might return with Locke to that starting place for constructive analysis which he called a state of nature. It was, by definition, a state of "perfect freedom . . . within the bounds of the law of nature."

A state also of equality, wherein all the power and jurisdiction is reciprocal, no one having more than another; there being nothing more evident than that creatures of the same species and rank, promiscuously born to all the same advantages of nature and the use of the same faculties, should also be equal one amongst another without subordination or subjection. . . .[5]

Because of this natural equality of men, no man could legitimately claim superiority over his fellow man. However, once the desirability of government was agreed upon, it was necessary that decisions be made, even though individuals of equal status disagreed. The only legitimate way in which a political system based upon the natural equality of man could arrive at decisions, Locke reasoned, was by majority rule. That is, he wrote, "every man, by consenting with others to make one body politic under one government, puts himself under an obligation to every one of that society to submit to the determination of the majority, and to be concluded by it. . . ." It is this view of the fundamental equality of man that at once necessitates and legitimatizes majority rule. Majority rule in turn derives its support from its equalitarian base. It is quite natural, therefore, for those who fear a "leveling equalitarianism" generally to be apprehensive of majority rule. It is also natural for those who seek an elevating equalitarianism to see in majority rule the appropriate instrument for its achievement.

For all that John Locke found no difficulty in defending both property rights and majority rule, American political theorists have tended to see in these two concepts a fundamental incompatibility, an inherently constant source of conflict. Indeed, most of the leading figures in the history of American political thought, as far as their theories dealt with the organization of government, have dedicated their energies to devising systems which avoided the imagined consequences of majority rule while preserving some semblance of its existence.

In general, four approaches have been employed to curb majority rule. The first, applicable to whites until nearly 1860, and still applicable in some areas of the South to Negroes in 1960, sought to reduce membership in the political majority through a restricted franchise. This was the intended function of the pre-Civil War white franchise, further restricted to property owners.

A second approach, employed by the framers of the Constitution and applicable in large measure until the Seventeenth Amendment was passed, restricted the number and kinds of offices which could be filled by those directly elected by a popular majority. The federal judiciary was removed from any electoral control; the Presidency was almost equally removed, selected as it was by electors who were appointed by state legislators who were themselves, finally, popularly elected.

Senators were elected by the state legislatures. The only popularly elected branch of the government, the House of Representatives, comprised in effect but one-fourth of the vital units of the national government, easily checked by the other three. The allocation of terms of office was also significant, the longest tenure ("good behavior") going to appointed judges, a tenure of four to six years to those indirectly elected, and a short two-year term to those popularly elected.

The rise of political parties seeking to organize national majorities broke down the electoral college curb early in the nineteenth century so that the Presidency became a nationally elected office; early in the twentieth century the U.S. Senate was brought under the control of popular majorities in the states. In all, the course of American history has brought greater coherence and control to popular majority rule. Thus the second restrictive approach has also failed.

The third restrictive approach to majority rule, the Madisonian approach, so parceled out power among governmental units that it seemed inconceivable that a coalition of factions could ever form a durable majority. Jealousies inherent in the office would motivate the officeholder to resist the aggrandizement of power at his expense by others; the separation of the units of government through the federal system, as well as the separation of powers, increased the difficulties of achieving a homogeneous majority of power, while at the same time it increased the prospects for parochial control of many of these units by opposing interests or factions. The units of state government were thus pitted against each other as well as against units of the national government; within the state, counties and districts were set against each other, for example, to control the legislature; and within the counties and districts were the opposing forces of interests and factions. By dividing and subdividing the majority, by turning it against itself, Madisonian theorists hoped to render it harmless.[6]

Judicial review of legislation also falls into this category of restraints, in that, in its classic justification by Hamilton in

Federalist number 78, it is portrayed not as elevating the judiciary over the legislature but as protecting the people from the untoward actions of majorities in their popularly elected legislatures. "It only supposes that the power of the people is superior to both [the judiciary and the legislature]. And that when the will of the legislature, declared in its statutes, stands in opposition to that of the people, declared in the Constitution, the judges ought to be governed by the latter rather than the former." [7]

A fourth restrictive approach, which is really a variation of the third, also pits power against power and constituency against constituency but does not leave this matter to chance. A deliberate construction of the legislature is employed so that the low-income majority is represented separately from the propertied minority. This theory finds its classic expression in John Adams's mixed or balanced government. In his system property qualifications would be required both for officeholding and for voting. However, lower property qualifications would be required for members of the state house of representatives than for the senate, and lower property qualifications would be required for the franchise to vote in elections for the house than in elections for the senate. Thus different classes would be represented in the different houses of the legislature. Calhoun subsequently developed this approach into a kind of functional representative system for minorities. This fourth restrictive approach, when combined with the third, appears frequently today in discussions of state legislative reapportionment.

To a very large extent the distrust of majority rule in early American political thought rested upon several closely related assumptions which were a part of the thinking of the age. It was an age which saw Europe still emerging from the fetters of feudalism, an age which saw the publication, in 1793, of Thomas Malthus's gloomy *Essay on Population*, a book destined to trouble the thinking of men for generations. It was an age in which men might easily assume that poverty and ignorance were inevitable in society; that virtue was related to property ownership; that the poor and ignorant would constitute a majority of the people, and that an unchecked majority would take for its members the property of the minority. It was not unnatural, therefore, for John Adams, brooding in England during the 1780's, to incorporate these assumptions into his thinking when he wrote his ponderous, three-volume *A Defense of the Constitutions of Government of the United States* (1787). What Adams was defending was the "mixed government" system, a balance of classes in the legislature found in some of the state constitutions (Massachusetts, in particular), against the claims of the Frenchman Turgot and the English critic Marchmont Nedham that the people were the best guardians of their liberties, and these liberties could best be protected through unfettered majority rule. In answering these critics, indignation, sarcasm, and passion showed through Adams's normally stolid prose as he affirmed his acceptance of the assumptions of the age.

Suppose a nation, rich and poor, high and low, ten millions in number, all assembled together; not more than one or two millions will have lands, houses or any personal property; if we take into the account the women and children, or even if we leave them out of the question, a great majority of every nation is wholly destitute of property except a small quantity of clothes and a few trifles of other movables. Would Mr. Nedham be responsible that if all were to be decided by a vote of the majority, the eight or nine millions who have no property would not think of usurping over the rights of the one or two millions who have? Property is surely a right of mankind as really as liberty. Perhaps, at first, prejudice, habit, shame or fear, principle or religion would restrain the poor from attacking the rich, and the idle from usurping on the industrious; but the time would come and pretexts be invented by degrees to countenance the majority in dividing all the property among them, or at least in sharing it equally with its present possessors. Debts would be abolished first; taxes laid heavy on the rich, and not at all on the others; and at last a downright equal division

of everything be demanded and voted. What would be the consequences of this? The idle, the vicious, the intemperate would rush
into the utmost extravagance of debauchery, sell and spend all
their share, and then demand a new division of those who purchased from them.[8]

One wonders, in retrospect, how John Adams failed to grasp
the significance of the differences in the property relationships,
as well as in the general standards of living, of the colonies in
comparison with those of the mother country. In 1764 Joseph
Trumbull of Connecticut visited Liverpool and wrote home
his impressions of the contrast in living conditions. "We in
New England know nothing of Poverty and want," he noted,
"we have no idea of the thing, how much better do our poor
people than ⅞ of the people of this much Famed Island." [9]

Recent research confirms the existence of a wide diffusion
of property in the colonial Massachusetts of Adams's day.
"While it is true that property ownership was a prerequisite
for province and town voting," Robert Brown has written, "it
is also true that the amount of property required for the
franchise was very small and that the great majority of men
could easily meet the requirements." [10] This view has been
confirmed by another study, which concludes that "in the
history of colonial suffrage and elections, contests arose more
frequently than might be expected from matters involving religion, ethnic, and national origins rather than from the issue of
property per se. With property so widely diffused, differences
and distinctions of other kinds appeared more significant." [11]
Yet Adams, obsessed with his fear of the impoverished masses,
failed to note the fundamental economic difference between
England and America and projected a theory which, in view of
the social conditions of the times, was actually more appropriate
to the former country than to the latter.

Adams's fear of majority rule and the propertyless masses
has lived on in American politics, however, for all that it was
not soundly grounded in economic fact. When in 1820 the
Massachusetts Constitutional Convention reconsidered the issue

41974

of property in politics and the nature of majority rule, the Adams system of "mixed government" was defended in principle. What, asked such worthies as Daniel Webster, Josiah Quincy, and Samuel Hoar, was the point of bicameralism if different classes were not to be represented in the different branches of the legislature? In opposition, reformers like Thomas Lincoln maintained that "Our government is one of the people, not a government of property. . . . Were it not for a government of the people, the people would be without property." [12] In the New York Constitutional Convention, meeting the following year, the noted jurist James Kent, whose *Commentaries on American Law* were to be a text to subsequent generations of law students, defended property qualifications for the suffrage, with the argument:

There is a constant tendency in human society, and the history of every age proves it; there is a tendency in the poor to covet and to share the plunder of the rich; in the debtor to relax or avoid the obligations of contracts; in the majority to tyrannize over the minority, and trample down their rights; in the indolent and the profligate to cast the whole burdens of society upon the industrious and the virtuous. . . .

Society is an association for the protection of property as well as of life, and the individual who contributes only one per cent to the common stock, ought not to have the same power and influence in directing the property concerns of the partnership, as he who contributes his thousands.[13]

But the actual balance of politics was against the conservatives, and the restrictive property qualifications for voting were removed from the state constitutions.

Although at the start of the American Revolution all of the states except Pennsylvania provided for property qualifications for the suffrage, by 1800 only eight of the original states continued such restrictions. In 1840 four states had property qualifications, and within a decade they, too, abandoned them. Yet the underlying theory that there was a fundamental conflict of interest between the majority of the people on the one hand

and a property-holding minority on the other continued. In 1842, some two decades after Massachusetts had departed from its property qualification for the suffrage, a Boston conservative Samuel Jones wrote *A Treatise of the Right of Suffrage* in which he appealed for the reinstatement of this provision.

The owners of property therefore have a deep interest in the affairs of the government; and an interest, too, which others have not. It is reasonable that they should have an influence and an agency in the government, in some degree commensurable with their interests. It may be emphatically asked, why persons having no property should have a right to interfere, by their votes, in the disposition of the property of others; or in the election of legislators and public officers whose most important duties are exercised in matters involving the rights of property? . . .

It should be kept in mind, that the owners of real estate have all the personal and other rights possessed by others; and it seems but just that they should have an additional influence, in public affairs, equal to their additional rights as owners of the whole territory of the country. And the public good most evidently requires that they should have this additional influence. They, as a class, combine, in the greatest degree, all those qualifications which entitle them to the confidence of the whole body of the people; and which furnish the best guaranty that they will always give their suffrages, intelligently and honestly, and under the influence of patriotic motives. And why should they not? The whole country is their own.[14]

❊

With the Jacksonian era came a new enthusiasm for equal rights. This feeling was manifested in the institution of national nominating conventions for the selection of party candidates for the Presidency, the extended suffrage, and the popular election of Presidential electors, bringing the executive branch of the national government within the reins of majority rule. Even as these fundamental changes were occurring, it was evident that there were deep sectional strains in American politics which portended a catastrophic cleavage between a sectional majority and a sectional minority. To John C. Calhoun of South Carolina it seemed that a new approach to American politics was needed, one which recognized the awesome role of national political parties in consolidating the powers of government—state and national, legislative, executive, and judicial —which the framers of the Constitution thought they had so permanently separated. Such an analysis ought furthermore to restate the case for the minority against the rising tide of majoritarianism. This Calhoun undertook to do in *A Disquisition on Government*, a work of rare lucidity for a treatise in political thought, for all that it left to mankind that imponderable term, the "concurrent majority." Before turning to Calhoun's argument, however, we should first review briefly some of the political factors which lay behind it.

Along with other Southern states during the 1820's, South Carolina felt an economic squeeze from the rapid growth in population and industry which took place in the Northern and Western states during that decade. The protective tariff, it was charged, favored industry at the expense of agriculture, and the South, economically dependent upon its sales of cotton, felt that the protective tariff laws of 1824 and 1828 were particularly harmful to it. Since some 82 per cent of the cotton grown at this time was exported, the South sought to lower the tariff as a necessary condition of its economic survival. Unable to curb a majority in Congress which favored a high tariff, South Carolina, led by Calhoun, in 1828 drew up the *South Carolina Exposition* which announced the doctrine of nullification. It was this doctrine, and the constitutional theory behind it, which was articulated by South Carolina's Senator Hayne in his famous debate with Webster in 1829–30. In 1832 another tariff bill was passed over Southern opposition, and a convention in South Carolina declared that the new tariff was "null, void, and no law, nor binding upon this State, its officers or citizens." The following year, Congress modified the tariff and another South Carolina convention repealed the nullification. Peace was thus restored, though at something of a price. The "next pretext," declared Andrew Jackson, "will be the Negro, or slavery question." [15]

The issue of slavery did not become a significant political question in American politics until the Missouri Compromise. From then until the Civil War, however, it took on ever increasing importance, as new lands were opened in the West and immigration helped swell population in the North. From 1820 to 1860, the Southern states felt themselves increasingly beleaguered by the opposition of a Northern and Western sectional majority on two vital questions of public policy: the tariff and slavery. Both questions basically affected the power structure in the South; yet the South held a position of diminishing power in Congress. This is not to suggest that Southern Congressmen were not firmly entrenched in power in Washington or in the Democratic party councils; it is only to observe that, with the rise of immigration in the North and the admission of new states in the West, the ante-bellum South was doomed to be a sectional minority with a proportionately smaller voice in national policy after each apportionment of Congress. This may be seen in the following table which shows the actual and proportional strength of the South in Congress in the years indicated.

CONGRESSIONAL REPRESENTATION OF THE SOUTH: 1840–60 *

Year	Southern Senators	Total Senate	Percentage South	Southern Representatives	Total House	Percentage South
1840	22	54	40.8	69	225	30.7
1850	22	62	35.5	66	234	27.4
1860	22	66	33.3	61	240	25.4

* The eleven states which subsequently constituted the Confederate States of America. Total House seats are those apportioned following the census of that year, counting only those states then admitted.

South Carolina was particularly hard hit by Congressional reapportionments, for between 1830 and 1860 it lost five seats in the House, so that it had only four seats remaining after the 1860 apportionment. When the last Southern state, Texas, was admitted into the Union in 1845, Calhoun set to work on his theory of the "concurrent majority."

Like John Adams and James Madison before him, Calhoun saw self-interest as the central motivating force in politics. Man, being a social animal, was forever impelled into society; yet being "so constituted that his direct or individual affections are stronger than his sympathetic or social feelings," he required government to control him. This, in turn, raised the problem of how a government strong enough to control the governed might itself be controlled so that the self-interest of the governors should not work to the abuse of the governed. John Adams had written of this classical political problem: "Self-interest, private avidity, ambition, and avarice, will exist in every state of society, and under every form of government." He had, therefore, been led to his solution of a mixed government, a system of separation of powers built upon separate classes. "The only remedy," he had written, "is to take away the power, by controlling the selfish avidity of the governor, by the senate and house; of the senate, by the governor and house; and of the house, by the governor and senate." [16]

This problem had equally vexed James Madison, when he observed that "the great difficulty lies in this: you must first enable the government to control the governed; and in the next place oblige it to control itself." [17] His solution, described in *Federalist* number 10, was to disperse factions over a wide territory and dilute their interests through the representative system. Furthermore, the separation of powers articulated in the U.S. Constitution would be a constitutional check upon the abuse of consolidated authority, for, he noted, "the great security against a gradual concentration of the several powers in the same department, consists in giving to those who administer each department the necessary constitutional means and

personal motives to resist encroachments of the others. . . .
Ambition must be made to counteract ambition. The interests
of the man must be connected with the constitutional rights of
the place." [18] It was in this familiar vein of thought that Calhoun examined the structure of government in the United
States in the late 1840's. "By what means," he wrote, "can government, without being divested of the full command of the
resources of the community, be prevented from abusing its
powers?" And, like his predecessors, he replied:

There is but one way in which this can possibly be done, and
that is by such an organism as will furnish the ruled with the
means of resisting successfully this tendency on the part of the
rulers to oppression and abuse. Power can only be resisted by
power—and tendency by tendency. Those who exercise power and
those subject to its exercise—the rulers and the ruled—stand in
antagonistic relations to each other.[19]

The assumption of antagonism between rulers and ruled
(which sounds rather like the abolitionist indictment of slavery) was understandable from the point of view of South
Carolina's declining position in national politics; it was hardly
an accurate description of the relationship between the government and the majority of those governed in the aftermath
of Jacksonian democracy. Calhoun's assumption of an antagonism between rulers and ruled turned upon a use of these
terms which was not made clear until he introduced the subject of the suffrage as a curb upon government. Then he
argued that the suffrage "can do no more than give complete
control to those who elect over the conduct of those who have
elected." The suffrage "transfers, in reality, the actual control
over the government from those who make and execute the
laws to the body of the community and thereby places the
powers of the government as fully in the mass of the community as they would be if they, in fact, had assembled, made,
and executed the laws themselves without the intervention of
representatives or agents." [20] The obvious difficulty for Cal-

houn was not that the rulers and ruled stood in an antagonistic relationship to each other but that, with the extension of the suffrage, they tended to be united; that is, in effect, the majority of the governed controlled the governors.

It was Calhoun's design to find some system to curb majority rule in fact while preserving it in form. To do this he coined the euphemistic phrase "concurrent majority." If individuals all had the same interests, if indeed the political community were homogeneous, he reasoned, there would be no need to fear majority rule (even, it may be added, as there would be no essential need for majority rule). However, interests varied with individuals. Calhoun therefore proposed that interests be considered as well as numbers, "considering the community as made up of different and conflicting interests, as far as the action of the government is concerned." [21] The sense of the community could thus be found through the organ of government representing interests, as well as through the organ representing what he called, tautologically, the "numerical majority."

Calhoun, it might be said, confounded a tautology with a euphemism to propound a conundrum. For what was the relevance of the numerical majority when it was denied the authority to execute its policies? In reality, Calhoun's "constitutional government" was but a thinly disguised form of minority rule. In his scheme of government the concurrent majority, representing a concurrence of interests as opposed to number, would be able by its veto power over the actions of the numerical majority, to curb majority rule when there was a conflict of interests between the two "majorities." By way of illustration of the concurrent majority system, Calhoun turned to the system of trial by jury in which unanimity was required for a verdict. Today, of course, one might illustrate Calhoun's system by pointing to the veto power of the charter member states in the U.N. Security Council. Having emasculated majority rule through the "concurrent majority" check, Calhoun could write, unabashedly: "Among the other advantages which governments of the concurrent have over those of the numerical majority—and which strongly illustrates their more popular character—is that they admit, with safety, a much greater extension of the right of suffrage. . . . There mere numbers have not the absolute control, and the wealthy and intelligent, being identified in interest with the poor and ignorant of their respective portions or interests of the community, become their leaders and protectors." [22]

John C. Calhoun was more than a passing spokesman for slavery and a cotton economy in an age of burgeoning industrialism, cheap immigrant labor, and continued continental expansion. He expressed, as had John Adams before him, the authentic voice of an alarmed conservativism which, seeing itself threatened by an irresistible majority, turns to technical devices in order to defend the *status quo*. Adams and Calhoun left a legacy which continues in American politics, rearticulated against each new effort to expand the scope of majority rule. The venerable concepts of the "balanced legislature" and the "concurrent majority" are still alive in many state legislative chambers today, as indeed are many of the essential assumptions about the social and economic order which once troubled John Adams and John C. Calhoun.

When one returns, however, to the fundamental assumptions which underlay much of the early distrust of majority rule in America, it becomes appropriate to inquire to what extent these assumptions are relevant to contemporary discussions. The poverty and ignorance that were once assumed to be inevitable in every society are not attributes of the majority in affluent, literate America. While poverty has certainly not been eliminated from society, no recent study has found that the poor constitute a majority of our population by any standard.[23] A political theory based upon the assumed poverty of the majority in America today is simply unrealistic; it would be equally unrealistic to base a theory on the presumed ignorance of the majority. Nor is the early assumption that the majority would be without property in any way supported by today's facts. In 1960 some 60 per cent of all American families held property in its most firmly established conservative form: home ownership.

There is some reason for saying that majority rule, far from being in conflict with property rights, has proved, in America at least, to be an indispensable condition for the protection of property. Only in those countries where majority rule has not been able to shape public policy so that the opportunities for the diffused acquisition of property were continually increased has property been genuinely insecure. The spread of private property has kept pace with the spread of effective majority rule. Yet it would not be true to say that majority rule has never voted away the property rights of a minority. There is the case of the abolition of slavery through the Thirteenth Amendment to the contrary.

The further charge that majority rule, proceeding as it does from an assumed ethic of equality, must conclude with a leveling equality of condition (a charge voiced by John Adams as well as by the critics of the Sixteenth Amendment) also seems hardly borne out by the American experience. One might assume from the criticism of the income tax amendment at the time it was suggested at the turn of the last century, or even some sixty years later, that such a public policy was ample demonstration of the leveling equalitarianism of majority rule and that it would result in the eradication of income differences. Many of these same charges were also leveled at the social legislation of the New Deal. Yet in a recent study of income distribution in the United States, published some three decades after the advent of the New Deal and a half century after the passage of the Sixteenth Amendment, quite different conclusions were found. For example, Gabriel Kolko wrote:

Most recent studies of American society assume that since the end of the Great Depression, in 1939, the nation's wealth has been redistributed and prosperity has been extended to the vast majority of the population. . . . But this assumption is nonetheless fallacious, for despite the obvious increase in prosperity since the abysmal years of the Great Depression, the basic distribution of income and wealth in the United States is essentially the same now as it was in 1939, or even 1910. Most low-income groups live substantially better today, but even though their real wages have mounted, their percentage of the national income has not changed.[24]

Contrary to Adams's assumption, it could be said today that not the minority were property owners, but the majority; and not the majority were poor, but a minority. Majority rule had eliminated neither poverty nor wealth. Rather than finding equality of income, Kolko found a third of the families living on "incomes too meager to provide minimum standards of health and decency," this during the prosperity of the 1950's. At the other extreme he found that, "Throughout the 1950's, the income of the top tenth was larger than the total for the bottom five income-tenths—about the same relationship as existed in 1910 and 1918." [25] In 1963, even as extreme conservatives were urging the repeal of the income tax amendment, the Internal Revenue Service reported that in 1961 more Americans reported incomes of a million dollars or more than in any year since 1929; and unofficial estimates placed the number of millionaires at several hundreds of thousands.[26] The leveling effect of majoritarian legislation was thus open to question.

The assumptions on which so many of the late eighteenth- and early nineteenth-century theorists based their fears of majority rule have been in many cases belied by the American experience. In the final analysis, the best argument against these antimajoritarian assumptions is to be found in any recent issue of the *Statistical Abstract*.

❊

In the twentieth century, as Arthur N. Holcombe pointed out some years ago, there was a political shift toward a class-oriented politics, away from the sectional politics which had characterized much of the past.[27] Today, with the rise of the urban majority, there is a blending of sectional and class politics with the densely populated, urbanized areas leaning in one direction and the more thinly populated, less urbanized areas leaning in another. Urbanization has modified the old contrasts of North and South, even as it has, through a combination of rising income and increasing public services, blurred class lines. Atlanta, St. Louis, San Francisco, and Philadelphia have more similarities as a result of their common character as heavily urbanized areas than they have differences as a result of their sectional location. Dallas has far more in common with Dayton, Ohio, than it has with Pecos County, Texas.

Urbanization introduced a new dimension into discussion of majority rule. When Adams and Calhoun wrote, an overwhelming rural majority was firmly entrenched in political power. Discussions of majority rule then were not confused, as they subsequently became, with issues of rural or urban biases and mythology. Late in the nineteenth century, however, it became evident that urban America posed a threat to rural America. In its nativistic aspects, the Populist revolt at the turn of the century represented in part the rural reaction to this threat.[28]

Though the farm belt failed to capture the Presidency, it did gain control of the organization of Congress. The last year in which rural America held a majority in the census figures, 1910, was also the year in which Senator Norris of Nebraska successfully led a revolt against the power of the Speaker in House committee appointments, thereby securing the seniority system as the basis for selection of House committee chairmanships. When the Census of 1920 revealed that rural America was in the minority, this not unexpected news still proved to be so politically disturbing that for the only time in our history Congress failed to reapportion itself following the census. Congress did, however, pass the Quota Law of 1921, the first restrictive immigration statute based upon a quota system of national origins. Obviously, not only would such restrictive immigration preserve the character of the national constituency in terms of national origins, but it would further curb the influx of immigrants generally into the urban areas. When, in 1929, Congress passed a reapportionment act to take effect after the 1930 census, it was evident why there had been a delay of two decades, for under the reapportionment some 26 seats were lost to 21 states. Twenty-one of these seats were lost in the rural South and Midwest. This substantial loss of seats, however, was offset in part by the rise of coalition politics in Congress and the seniority system of committee chairmanships. The net effect, for the next three decades, was no real loss in power for the rural constituency, for what was lost in the census was regained under the Rules of the House and in the composition of state legislatures.

Closely associated with the long political hegemony of rural America had been a mythology, whether based on fact or fancy, of the rural way of life as central to the proper scheme of values. Much of the mythology has an ancient lineage reaching beyond the earliest American settlements to arguments heard in ancient Greece and early Rome. In America these arguments were strengthened by the authority of the ever quotable Jefferson, who had observed in a memorable passage in his *Notes On Virginia:*

Those who labour in the earth are the chosen people of God, if ever He had a chosen people, whose breasts He had made His peculiar deposit for substantial and genuine virtue.

And further, in a letter to John Jay:

Cultivators of the earth are the most valuable citizens. They are the most vigorous, the most independent, the most virtuous, and they are tied to their country, and wedded to its liberty and interests by the most lasting bonds.[29]

It was, of course, to be expected that such a view would appear both reasonable and popular in eighteenth-century America when urbanized communities constituted less than 5 per cent of the population. But the tenacity of the myth was indeed remarkable, for even as the face of America changed with ever increasing industrialization throughout the nineteenth century, the myth was reiterated in popular novels and political speeches. At mid-century, in 1851, Representative George W. Julian of Indiana said: "The life of a farmer is peculiarly favorable to virtue; and both individuals and communities are generally happy in proportion as they are virtuous." [30] At the end of the century the Wisconsin historian, Frederick Jackson Turner, offered a tribute to both the frontier and the rural majority when he wrote in a titanic sentence:

European men, institutions and ideas were lodged in the American wilderness, and this great American West took them to her bosom, taught them a new way of looking upon the destiny of the common man, trained them in adaptation to the conditions of the New World, to the creation of new institutions to meet new needs; and ever as society on her eastern border grew to resemble the Old World in its social forms and its industry, ever, as it began to lose faith in the ideal of democracy, she opened new provinces, and dowered new democracies in her most distant domains with her material treasures and with the ennobling influence that the fierce love of freedom, the strength that came from hewing out a home, making a school and a church, and creating a higher future for his family, furnished to the pioneer.[31]

Behind the myth of inherent rural virtue there recur certain assumptions which have lingered on well after the passing of the frontier and the rural majority, and which have become a part of political discussions on reapportionment and the balance of power today. In 1930, Professor Wilson Gee wrote a book entitled, *The Place of Agriculture in American Life*, for the World Today Bookshelf (at the request of Charles A. Beard who was chairman of the board of editors of the series). Professor Gee, a rural economist and rural sociologist, while noting that "knowledge of the field is incomplete, and often a matter of opinion," felt constrained to offer the following traits as distinctive of rural life.

There is nothing so characteristic of the farmer as his *individualism*. . . .

Conservatism at times greatly irritates the progressive elements in society, but it has often kept the world from running amuck. And the farmer is notably a conservative.

The farmer vote is generally conceded to be a more thoughtful vote than the heterogeneous city vote. . . .

A recent study by the author tends to confirm the existing opinion that *thrift* and *frugality* are virtues more prevalent in the country than in the city. . . .

Nowhere else as in the country is there exhibited a like *democracy* of attitude. . . .

The farmer is the most *religious* element of our population. . . .

The very foundations of our civilization are laid in the *sacredness of the family ties*. . . . Statistics show that there is a larger proportion of divorces in the city than in the country. . . .

The chief danger in the cityward drift is that we may fail to carry over into our new urban majority those country characteristics that have made our national life great. The city environment can never foster independence of action, conservatism, democracy of attitude, thrift and frugality, religiosity, and the strength and purity of family life as does the country. . . .[32]

Some thirty years after these lines were written, when the urban majority had moved from 56 to 70 per cent of the population, this view was still significant in American politics.

The obvious corollary to the myth that rural areas provide the national seedbed of public and private virtue has been the venerable belief that the city is a center of corruption, a veritable den of iniquity. The rural-urban conflict may be seen, according to the myth, as something in the way of an eternal and titanic struggle between the forces of good and evil. "The mobs of great cities," Jefferson wrote, "add just so much to the support of pure government, as sores do to the strength of the human body." And in another passage he left this awesome prophecy: "I think our governments will remain virtuous for many centuries; as long as they are chiefly agricultural; and this will be as long as there shall be vacant lands in any part of America. When they get piled up upon one another in large cities, as in Europe, they will become corrupt as in Europe." [33]

By the end of the nineteenth century, when Frederick Jackson Turner had signalized the closing of the frontier with his memorable essay on its significance in history, many Americans felt that Jefferson's prophecy had come to pass, as exposures in city after city revealed mounting evidence that city politics were at odds with traditional American ideals. Yet to the native rural American it was not alone the city that threatened his way of life; even more so it was the foreigner with his alien language, customs, and religion. What seemed to be at stake was not only rural Protestant America but civilization itself; thus the American Home Missionary Society advertised in 1887 "Save America To Save the World." [34]

In an effort to "save America" the American Home Missionary Society published a little book entitled *Our Country* by the Reverend Josiah Strong, of the Home Missions in Ohio. The book was an immediate commercial success, for it had the backing of over a thousand Home Missions, and by the time of the revised edition in 1890 the publishers could claim a distribution of 168,000 copies. It was Strong's contention that the Anglo-Saxon was the representative of two great ideas: civil liberty and spiritual Christianity. He was, therefore, "divinely commissioned to be, in a peculiar sense, his brother's keeper"; [35] that is, unless the Anglo-Saxon failed to weather the various "perils" which beset him, caused by immigration. "It is immigration which has fed fat the liquor power; and there is a liquor vote. Immigration furnishes most of the victims of Mormonism; and there is a Mormon vote. Immigration is the strength of the Catholic church; and there is a Catholic vote. Immigration is the mother and nurse of American socialism; and there is to be a socialist vote. Immigration tends strongly to the cities, and gives to them their political complexion. And there is no more serious menace to our civilization than our rabble-ruled cities." [36] By a curious computation Strong arrived at the conclusion that in 1880, while less than a third of the total population was foreign by birth or parentage, this category included some 62 per cent of the population of Cincinnati, 63 per cent of Boston, 83 per cent of Cleveland, 88 per cent of New York and 91 per cent of Chicago. "There are wards in New York and other large cities," he wrote, "where there is but one Protestant church to every ten or fifteen thousand souls: which means that those wards are from one-twentieth to one-thirtieth as well supplied with churches as the whole land. In Ohio, even including the cities, more than one-fifth of the population is in Evangelical churches. . . ." [37]

Clearly, the Reverend Josiah Strong, for all of his provinciality and nativism, expressed an outlook that was not uncommon in rural America late in the nineteenth century. Immigration, industrialization, and urbanization had altered the pattern of American politics, and soon the rural majority would become the minority. "We must face the inevitable," Strong wrote in *The Twentieth Century City* (1898). "The new civilization is certain to be urban; and the problem of the twentieth century will be the city." Nearly a decade later, in *The Challenge of the City* (1907), Strong revised the message to get to the nub of the matter. "We must face the inevitable," he now wrote. "It is only a question of time when the greater part of our population will be urban, and our cities will possess all the power which in a democracy belongs to majorities." [38]

The myth of the dichotomy of rural virtue and urban vice has continued in American politics, for it has been articulated not only by farm groups and small-town businessmen, but by conservative urban forces who have sought to hold off state welfare legislation by keeping the urban reformers districted into a legislative minority. When urban reform groups have reiterated the familiar demands of "no taxation without representation" and "one man, one vote," they have been frequently met with embellishments on the theme that "the farmer is the backbone of American democracy," and "American democracy requires 'balanced' legislatures."

In 1949 the Conference of Mayors made an effort to call to

the attention of the public the need for state legislative reapportionments. They pointed out that at that time, for example, 48 per cent of the people in California lived in Los Angeles and San Francisco, yet they were allocated only 5 per cent of the seats in the upper house of the California legislature. In other words, the vote of a resident of Los Angeles or San Francisco for a member of the upper house was worth only one-tenth of the vote of the rural resident. In response to the statement of the Conference of Mayors, the nationally syndicated columnist Roger W. Babson addressed an article to his readers, who he noted "are largely people in the smaller communities." While conceding the fact of unequal apportionment in the states, Babson declared, "I insist that the present setup is in the interest of Good Government. Rural people have better character and much more time to think and read than do large city people. The children of rural people are today supplying the best citizens for the large cities. The vote of people in small cities and rural communities should count more than the vote of the ordinary city man." Babson then went on to review the vices of the city in much the same vein as had Josiah Strong late in the nineteenth century. In the city were to be found poverty, welfare expenditures, gangsters, and immorality. "Most big city voters are ignorant people," he declared. "They know nothing about Government and are largely controlled by unscrupulous ward heelers." Therefore, he advised his readers to "insist on continuing the apportionment setups of today."

One Michigan legislator, Senator A. P. Decker, was so impressed with Roger Babson's article that he reprinted it on a handbill for distribution throughout the state when the question of reapportionment came up there in 1950. He added a postscript to it, however. "There are 32 Senators in the State Senate," he noted. "Seven of these are from Wayne Co. [Detroit], of which 2 are Michigan-born and 5 born outside the State. . . . In the rest of the State, known as the 'sticks,' the 17 Senators remaining, show 15 Michigan-born and 2 born outside the state." The House of Representatives, with 100 members, had 27 from Wayne County [Detroit]. "Of this 27, only 9 are Michigan-born while 18 were born outside the state. The rest of the House comprises 73 members and 60 of these are Michigan-born with 13 born outside the State." Thus was the traditional suspicion of immigrants carried to a rare extreme of parochial xenophobia.[39]

The presence of an urban majority, in national politics as well as in half the states, has joined the issue of majority rule to the issue of urban rule. Initially, the issue of majority rule was considered in a rural context, but along what were at bottom lines of class interest. In Calhoun's day, with the population still approximately 90 per cent rural, majority rule was considered in the context of essentialy sectional alignments. Today these arguments against majority rule have been joined with an equally traditional fear of urban politics and the imagined consequences of unchecked urban domination. The appeal for a rural constituency curb on urban constituency power, either through area representation in one house and popular representation in the other or through ingenious cartography to balance the urban and rural districts, thus draws upon a long and strong heritage in American politics.

❋

When it is remembered that the Supreme Court case overturning racial segregation in the public schools was decided nearly a decade ago, it cannot be expected that the apportionment case of *Baker v. Carr* will work any immediately apparent revolution in our political system, though in the long run its consequences should prove equally significant. For decades the typical pattern of state legislative politics in much of the country (outside the South) has tended to produce a division between rural-oriented Republicans and urban-oriented Democrats. This has led to woeful political results in many of the states, results which reach much further than the frequent deadlock between a senate based largely on area representation and a house system based roughly on population. It has led to a tendency toward rigidity in state politics itself. For instance, a recent study of the Michigan House of Representatives from 1954 to 1961 showed that during this period 102 of the 110 seats "or 92 per cent were won by the same party in all four elections." [40] With nearly even division between Republicans and Democrats in the house, most of the representatives from each party came from "safe or solid" districts: 81.3 per cent of the Republicans, 76.7 per cent of the Democrats. Stable one-party districts thus emerged as the typical pattern of Michigan House politics. And within these districts there was very little competition in the party primaries; however, where it did exist it tended to be in urban districts.

When these districts were analyzed in terms of rural-urban classifications, it was found that the Democrats were dominant in the urban areas, the Republicans in the rural areas, with the most competition between the parties taking place in mixed rural-urban districts. The impact of this alignment on public policy proved to be significant indeed. For, when selected roll call votes were analyzed in terms of liberal and conservative categories, it was found that 75.4 per cent of the Republicans voted "conservative" at least 90 per cent of the time, while 75.5 per cent of the Democrats voted "liberal" at least 90 per cent of the time.[41] So in Michigan, as in many other states, pronounced political alignments set off rural Republican conservatives on the one hand and urban Democratic liberals on the other. With a predominantly urban and mixed urban-rural population in the state, this has meant that the rural minority has maintained its disproportionate power in the house by effectively resisting plans for an equitable reapportionment. The representation in the state senate was sufficiently distorted so that in 1958, 47 per cent of the voters (Republicans) elected 65 per cent of the members.[42] Reapportionment of state legislatures, in both houses, could be expected therefore to produce a reorientation of state politics, making them more genuinely competitive, as well as tending to bring the party politics of legislatures into harmony with members of their party in the executive branch of government, elected from a statewide constituency.

The consequences of state legislative reapportionments, however, should reach well beyond the state level of politics and into the Congressional House of Representatives, where there is equally an imbalance of political strength between urban and rural districts (districts laid out by the state legislatures) and a lack of harmony on policies between the executive and legislative branches. In general, rural Congressional districts tend to be noncompetitive districts, both within the incumbent party and between parties.[43] One-party districts make possible seniority in Congress; seniority in Congress makes inevitable committee chairmanships. Congressional committee chairmanships fall largely to Southern or Border-State Congressmen when the Democrats are in power, and to Midwesterners when the Republicans are in power. The usually more competitive politics of the urban areas tend to deny committee chairmanships to urban Congressmen. For example, in 1962, the ten most populous states, which contained over half the population of the country, provided no committee chairmen in the Senate, and only two ranking members of the sixteen Senate committees. Arizona, New Mexico, Arkansas, Virginia, and Maryland, however, each provided two Senators who were either committee chairmen or ranking members. Rural districts and rural states thus largely control Congressional committees in urban America.

Gerrymandering, as has often been remarked, is as old as the republic. A map of Congressional districts looks like a black and white drawing of a very mad abstractionist. But there is, of course, nothing mad about it at all; every line has its purpose, and behind the purpose is political power. For the party which controls the state legislature is able to hobble its opponents in the race for Congressional seats. The districting achieved by state legislatures has led to some highly interesting results, as witness the composition of the state of New York's 43 Congressional districts. In the 87th (1960) Congress, New York was represented by 21 Republicans and 22 Democrats. If, however, we rank the Republican and Democratic districts in terms of the density of population per square mile, as an index of the urban conditions of living in these districts, we see immediately how the parties draw upon different constituencies. In the accompanying table it will be seen that only three Republican districts (4, 25, 17) have the problem of density of population encountered in the typical Democratic district, while only three Democratic districts (32, 30, 1) have the relative sparseness of population encountered in the typical Republican district. The spacious 33rd district which sprawls through five counties at the Canadian border is Republican; the incredibly crowded 18th district in Harlem is Democratic. The densely packed city districts, where the problems of congested living are most acute, are Democratic; the more thinly populated districts, where the problems of congested living are not ever-present, are Republican. Except for the six districts noted above, one could rank all the Congressional districts of New York in the 87th Congress in terms of density of population and, using 6,500 per square mile as the cut-off point, give all below that mark to the Republicans, all above it to the Democrats, and closely approximate the actual results.

Urbanization, as measured in the density of population, is altering many of the heretofore sectional patterns of American politics. In the Republican outposts of Maine, Vermont, Iowa, Kansas, and Nebraska, urbanization is producing Democrats; in the Democratic stronghold of the South, urbanization is producing Republicans. Urbanization has in this way facilitated the organization of an active and articulate opposition to the traditional party in power. In the Presidential election of 1960 the most densely populated districts in Kansas and Nebraska, for example, returned the lowest Republican margins in those states, while the most densely populated districts in Virginia, North Carolina, Alabama, Tennessee, and Texas went Repub-

NEW YORK CONGRESSIONAL ELECTION (1960), 87TH CONGRESS [44]

Republican		Democratic	
District	Pop. Density	District	Pop. Density
33	44.1	32	82.0
31	61.2	30	526.1
43	76.5	1	932.3
36	84.2	5	11,860.7
29	102.1	11	14,206.5
34	115.7	41	17,514.5
28	118.2	6	22,073.3
37	146.3	7	26,586.8
39	194.8	9	30,095.3
38	455.9	14	33,946.5
42	517.0	13	35,331.3
35	534.1	12	39,522.1
40	789.6	8	39,662.3
27	1,217.8	24	49,698.6
26	1,297.4	10	50,540.3
2	3,183.6	23	55,861.0
3	6,027.9	22	65,442.6
15	6,111.9	20	69,868.8
4	16,116.7	21	71,532.5
25	16,581.8	19	75,374.8
17	43,372.5	16	100,524.7
		18	134,684.0

lican. In North Carolina, the five most densely populated districts voted Republican, while five of the seven least densely populated districts stayed Democrat.

Even as urbanization is producing Republicans in the South, it is also producing more liberal Democrats there than those who have generally come from the more rural areas. This opposition of rural-urban politics was highlighted a few years ago when V. O. Key, Jr., wrote *Southern Politics* (1949). "That urbanization dilutes an agrarian regionalism," he noted, "is the most arresting fact emerging from analysis of the voting records of southern Democratic Representatives." [45] After analyzing twenty-eight roll-call votes on which a majority of

Southern Democrats joined with Republicans to vote against a majority of non-Southern Democrats, Key found that the results supported "the theory that it is from the southern urban centers that the northern Democrats are most likely to win allies when a majority of southerners vote with the Republicans." The higher the degree of urbanization in Southern Congressional districts, the greater was the likelihood of Southern Democratic representatives voting with their party elsewhere. Conversely, the more rural the Southern state, the greater the likelihood of its Democratic representatives voting with the Republicans.

This points again to the rural, agrarian basis for occasional southern Democratic coalitions with Republicans. This community of interest, from the nature of the issues involved, does not seem to rest chiefly on common economic interest. The economic interests of northern and southern agrarians as often as not conflict. The bond of unity rather, it may be suspected, wells from a shared antipathy toward urban people and perhaps a common lack of sympathetic understanding of the problems of an urban, industrial society." [46]

This urban-rural, liberal-conservative distinction seems not to be restricted to the South, but appears to permeate American politics generally. If we look at the voting records of New York's Congressmen in terms of the density of population of their districts, we find interesting results. On the eve of the Congressional election in 1962, the *Congressional Quarterly* reported the results of a study it had made of the 87th Congress, in which it listed the voting records of each member in terms of the times (in percentages) he had voted in support of, or in opposition to, the conservative coalition of Republicans and Southern Democrats on sixteen roll-call votes in 1962. [47] When we take the voting records of the Republican Congressmen from the five most sparsely populated districts, we find that they voted (when averaged) in support of the conservative coalition 73.8 per cent of the time and in opposition to it

7.4 per cent. (Failure to total 100 per cent here and below reflects failure to vote on all roll calls.) But, when we move into the five most densely populated Republican districts, we find the vote in support of the coalition only 46.2 per cent, opposing 43.6 per cent. When we shift to the five lowest density Democratic districts, we find their Congressmen voting in support of the conservative coalition 13.8 per cent, and opposing 77.4 per cent. But, when we take the five highest density Democratic districts, support of the coalition drops to 2.4 per cent and opposition rises to 86.8 per cent.

If we turn to neighboring New Jersey, the second-most densely populated state (806.7 per square mile, Rhode Island 812.4) and the most densely populated with a Republican Congressional delegation in the 87th Congress, and rank the Republican districts in terms of density of population, we also see some relationship of this factor to liberal and conservative voting.

NEW JERSEY REPUBLICAN DISTRICTS, 87TH CONGRESS [48]

District	Density of Pop. (per square mile)	Conservative Coalition Support (per cent)	Opposed (per cent)
2	235.2	44	44
7	353.6	50	50
3	462.4	69	31
1	650.7	37	56
5	764.2	37	56
12	4,269.6	31	69
9	4,748.7	37	63
6	4,895.7	25	75

While this pattern of voting behavior in relation to density of population is subject to the infinite variations of local and state political conditions, there would nevertheless appear to be sufficient evidence to indicate that with the increasing urbanization of America the density factor will take on increasing importance. The types of political questions that arise in the densely populated districts differ from those of the less congested areas and doubtless will continue to demand in the future, as they have in the past, different kinds of solutions. This means greater liberal thrust emanating from the more densely populated sections of the country, a continuation of the push for what many regard as the bare essentials of equality in American life. It has been the city, with its pluralism of religious belief, which has brought the equality of man—regardless of religious belief—to the fore in contemporary politics. It has been again the city, long the home of racial pluralism, which has revitalized the meaning of equality, regardless of race, in American life. "The whole thrust of today's legal climate is to end unconstitutional discrimination," wrote Judge McLaughlin in a recent apportionment case.[49] In giving new meaning to the "equal protection" clause of the Fourteenth Amendment, the Supreme Court has but taken cognizance of an urban majority which has been seeking to achieve that power in politics which it may democratically claim by virtue of its numbers.

This surge of equalitarianism in the mid-twentieth century marks a return to the principles enunciated in the Declaration of Independence, even as it marks a departure from traditional practice; it reasserts the ideological validity of John Locke, even as it rejects the systems of John Adams and John C. Calhoun. A theory of this equalitarian social revolution may be derived from our historical experience.

Traditionally, American politics has reflected in its principles the composition of its constituents. For much of our history the country has been predominantly Protestant and has reflected in its politics a Protestant prejudice, for all the intended separation of religion from the political affairs of men; the country has been predominantly white and has reflected in its politics a pattern of white supremacy; the country has been predominantly rural and has reflected in its politics this rural hegemony. The lack of a generally accepted standard for determining religious superiority in the presence of religious diversity fostered the equal acceptance of all men, notwithstanding their religion. The lack of a generally accepted standard for determining racial superiority in the presence of racial diversity leads similarly to universalizing the concept "equality of man," notwithstanding race. And the lack of a generally accepted standard for determining political superiority, whereby voters might be classified into inferior and superior constituents, leads to the equalitarian solution of giving equal votes to all voters. Public policies which have categorically discriminated among men because of their religion, race, or residence, through systems of classification based upon principles other than the equality of all individuals, have invariably produced antagonisms that, in one way or another, impaired the peace of the political community. In seeking to establish equality as the proper basis for majority rule, the country may be said to be approximating some of the ethical imperatives of the natural law heritage; this achievement, however, may also be said to mark the triumph of pragmatic liberalism in politics. For equality, long considered an idealistic concept in the tradition of democratic values, is today becoming a realistic solution to the problems of practical politics in our heterogeneous American society.

NOTES

1. 82 S. Ct. 691 (1962).
2. Charles L. Black, Jr. "The Proposed Amendment of Article V: A Threatened Disaster," *The Yale Law Journal*, 72 (Apr. 1963) 5, p. 960.
3. Gordon E. Baker, *Rural Versus Urban Political Power* (New York: Random House, Inc., 1955), p. 16. (Gordon E. Baker should not be confused with Charles W. Baker of *Baker v. Carr*.)
4. This table is an adaptation of Gordon E. Baker's comprehensive table which carries all of the then forty-eight states, presented in *op. cit.*, pp. 16–17.
5. John Locke, *Of Civil Government* (New York: Everyman's Library, 1924), p. 119.
6. See: Robert A. Dahl, *A Preface to Democratic Theory* (Chicago: The University of Chicago Press, 1956); James MacGregor Burns, *The Deadlock of Democracy* (Englewood Cliffs, N.J.: Prentice-Hall, Inc., 1963); Edwin Mims, Jr., *The Majority of the People* (New

York: Modern Age Books, 1941). H. S. Commager, *Majority Rule and Minority Rights* (New York: Oxford University Press, 1943); and the venerable J. Allen Smith, *The Spirit of American Government* (New York: The Macmillan Co., 1907).

7. *The Federalist* (New York: Tudor Publishing Co., 1937), p. 102.

8. *The Political Writings of John Adams*, George A. Peek, Jr., (ed.) (New York: The Liberal Arts Press, 1954), pp. 147-8.

9. Connecticut Historical Society, *Jonathan Trumbull Papers, 1746–1784*, in Chilton Williamson, *American Suffrage from Property to Democracy, 1760–1860* (Princeton, N.J.: Princeton University Press, 1960), p. 39.

10. Robert E. Brown, *Middle-Class Democracy and the Revolution in Massachusetts, 1691–1780* (Ithaca: Cornell University Press, 1955), p. 402.

11. Williamson, *op. cit.*, pp. 53-4.

12. *Journal of Debates and Proceedings in the Convention of Delegates Chosen To Revise the Constitution of Massachusetts, 1820*, new edition, revised and corrected (Boston: 1853), p. 265.

13. *Reports of the Proceeding and Debates of the Convention of 1821, Assembled for the Purpose of Amending the Constitution of the State of New York* (Albany: 1821), p. 22.

14. Samuel Jones, *A Treatise of the Right of Suffrage* (Boston: Otis, Broaders and Company, 1842), pp. 109, 114-15.

15. Samuel E. Morison and Henry S. Commager, *The Growth of the American Republic* (New York: Oxford University Press, 1958), Vol. I, p. 485.

16. *The Works of John Adams*, Charles Francis Adams (ed.) (Boston: Charles C. Little and James Brown, 1851), Vol. VI, pp. 57-8.

17. *The Federalist, op. cit.*, no. 51.

18. *Ibid.*

19. John C. Calhoun, *A Disquisition On Government*, C. Gordon Post (ed.) (New York: The Liberal Arts Press, 1953), p. 11.

20. *Ibid.*, p. 12.

21. *Ibid.*, p. 23.

22. *Ibid.*, pp. 35-6.

23. See: Michael Harrington, *The Other America* (New York: The Macmillan Company, 1962); Gabriel Kolko, *Wealth and Power in America* (New York: Frederick A. Praeger, 1962).

24. Kolko, *op. cit.*, p. 3.

25. *Ibid.*, pp. 4, 12-13.

26. *Lansing State Journal*, July 16, 1963, C-3.

27. See: A. N. Holcombe, *The New Party Politics* (1933), *The Middle Classes in American Politics* (1940).

28. See: Richard Hofstadter, *The Age of Reform* (New York: Vintage

Books, 1960), Chapter 2. Also see: Russell B. Nye, *Midwestern Progressive Politics* (East Lansing, Mich.: M.S.U. Press, 1951).

29. A. Whitney Griswold, *Farming and Democracy* (New Haven: Yale University Press, 1952), pp. 30–31.

30. Henry Nash Smith, *Virgin Land* (Cambridge: Harvard University Press, 1950), p. 171.

31. "The Significance of the Frontier in American History," in *ibid.*, p. 254.

32. Wilson Gee, *The Place of Agriculture in American Life* (New York: The Macmillan Company, 1930), pp. 10–22. Italics in original.

33. Griswold, *op. cit.*, pp. 30–31.

34. Advertisement following Index in Josiah Strong, *Our Country* (New York: The Baker & Taylor Co., n.d., 1885 edition but apparently 1887 printing).

35. *Ibid.*, p. 161.

36. *Ibid.*, p. 43.

37. *Ibid.*, p. 135.

38. Josiah Strong, *The Twentieth Century* (New York: The Baker and Taylor Co., 1898), p. 53, *The Challenge of the City* (New York: Eaton & Mains, 1907), p. 35.

39. The Roger Babson article together with Senator A. P. Decker's comments are reprinted in Charles M. Knier and Guy Fox, *Readings in Municipal Government and Administration* (New York: Rinehart & Company, 1953), pp. 127–9. There have been numerous illustrations of the fear of the urban alien in politics. Among the more extreme statements of this anxiety was that of a Tennessee editor George Fort Milton, who wrote of Al Smith's try for the Presidency that he appealed "to the alien, who feel that the older America, the America of the Anglo-Saxon stock, is a hateful thing which must be overturned and humiliated; to the northern Negroes, who lust for social equality and racial dominance; to the Catholics who have been made to believe that they are entitled to the White House and to the Jews who likewise are to be instilled with the feeling that this is the time for God's chosen people to chastise America [*sic*] yesteryear. . . ." Quoted in James MacGregor Burns, *The Deadlock of Democracy* (Englewood Cliffs, N.J.: Prentice-Hall, Inc., 1963), p. 151.

40. Robert Becker *et al.*, "Correlates of Legislative Voting: Michigan House of Representatives, 1954–1961," *Midwest Journal of Political Science*, 6 (1962) 4, p. 386.

41. "Liberalism and Conservatism are used here in the popular sense in which they refer to positive and negative attitudes toward governmental ownership, intervention, and regulation of the economy; measures for promoting equalitarianism and social welfare through government action; etc." *Ibid.*, p. 393.

42. See: Herbert Garfinkel and L. J. Fein, *Fair Representation: A Citizen's Guide to Legislative Apportionment in Michigan* (East Lansing. Bureau of Social and Political Research, Michigan State University, 1960), p. 13.

43. See: Joseph A. Schlesinger, "The Structure of Competition for Office in the American States," *Behavioral Science*, 5 (1960) 3 for the low competitive ranking of Congressional district politics generally.

44. Density of districts from *The Congressional District Data Book* (Districts of the 87th Congress), U.S. Department of Commerce, Bureau of the Census (Washington: U.S. Government Printing Office, 1961).

45. V. O. Key, Jr., *Southern Politics* (New York: Alfred A. Knopf, Inc., 1949), p. 378.

46. *Ibid.*, p. 380.

47. *Congressional Quarterly Weekly Report*, No. 44, Nov. 2, 1962, pp. 2072–3.

48. Density figures from *The Congressional Data Book, op. cit.*, conservative coalition support and opposition percentages from the *Congressional Quarterly Weekly Report, op. cit.*

49. *Dyer v. Kazuhisa Abe*, C. D., 138 F. Supp. 220, 236, cited by Justice Douglas in *Baker v. Carr*.

INDEX

Abolitionists, 49
Act of Toleration of 1649, 16, 17
Act of Toleration of 1689, 9, 20
Acts of Uniformity and Supremacy of 1559, 7
Adams, Alice Dana, 85 n.
Adams, Charles Francis, 127 n.
Adams, John, 98, 99, 100, 101, 105, 108, 109, 111, 125
Aldrich, Thomas Bailey, 64
Ali, Noble Drew, 66
A.F. of L., 61
American Home Missionary Society, 115
American Revolution, 18, 20-21, 25, 29, 44
Anabaptists, 9, 16, 23
Anglican Church, 8, 13, 21
Anti-Catholicism, 28, 29
Anti-Semitism, 28, 63, 65
Antinomians, 9, 16
Article Six, U.S. Constitution, 22, 23
Association of Citizens' Councils, 50, 53, 54
Autobiography of Thomas Jefferson, 48

Babson, Roger W., 117, 128 n.

Baker, Gordon E., 93, 126 n.
Baker v. Carr (1962), 89, 90, 91, 118
Baltimore, Lord, 13, 15, 16
Baptist Church, 18, 23, 34
Bartlett, John Russell, 40 n.
Becker, Robert, 128 n.
Bellarmine, Robert Cardinal, 38 n.
Berkeley, Governor, 13
Black, Charles L., Jr., 91, 126 n.
Black, Justice Hugo, 35
Book of Common Prayer, 7
Brady, Judge Tom P., 52, 54, 86 n.
Breedlove v. Suttles (1937), 71
Brennan, Justice, 89
Brown, Henry B., 57
Brown, Oliver, 75
Brown, Robert E., 100, 127 n.
Brown v. Board of Education, 50, 67, 75, 77, 78, 80, 81, 83, 88 n.
Brownell, Herbert, 75
Bunche, Ralph, 47
Burns, James MacGregor, 68, 88 n., 127 n., 128 n.
Byrd, William, 42-3, 85 n.

Calhoun, John C., 54, 98, 103, 105-8, 111, 125, 127 n.
Calvert, Cecil, 15

Calvin, John, 24, 38 n.
Calvinism, 9
Cannibals All, 54
Cartwright, Samuel A., 51
Catholic, *see* Roman Catholic Church
Catterall, Helen T., 85 n.
Challenge of the City, The, 116
Chambers, William, 48
Chinese, 60, 63
Chinese Exclusion Act, 61, 63
"Christian View on Segregation, A," 50
Civil Rights, 68, 69
Civil Rights Act of 1875, 57
Civil Rights Cases of 1883, 56
Civil Rights Section, Department of Justice, 69
Civil War, 29, 50, 55
Clark, Justice Tom, 90
Clarke, John, 19
Classic theory of religious liberty, 23-4, 26-7, 30, 31, 34, 36, 37
Clay, Henry, 46
Cobb, Sanford H., 38 n., 39 n.
Comas, Juan, 49, 86 n.
Commager, Henry S., 88 n., 127 n.
Commentaries on American Law, 101
"Concurrent majority," 103, 105, 107, 108
Conference of Mayors, 116, 117
Congregational Church, 12, 13, 23
Congress of Racial Equality, 81
Congressional Quarterly, 123
Contract labor system, 60
Corrigan v. Buckley (1926), 71-2
Cotton Is King, 52
Cotton, John, 8, 9, 10, 38 n.
Council of State Governments, 91
"Court of the Union," 91
Coxe, Tench, 23
Crallé, Richard K., 87 n.

Crèvecoeur, Hector St. John de, 25, 39 n.
Curti, Merle, 95

Dahl, Robert A., 127 n.
Davis, Hugh, 45
Davis, John W., 75
Decker, Senator A. P., 117, 128 n.
Declaration of Independence, 45, 47, 64, 85, 125
Defense of the Constitutions of Government of the United States, 99
Defense of Liberty Against Tyrants, A, 6
Democracy in America, 28
Detweiler, Philip F., 85 n., 86 n.
Disquisition on Government, A, 103
Douglas, Justice William O., 34, 40 n., 90
Drake, Samuel G., 85 n.
Dred Scott case, 75
DuBois, W.E.B., 66, 85 n.
Dudley, Thomas, 14

Eastland, Senator James O., 53, 87 n.
Ebenstein, William, 38 n.
Education and religion, 32, 33
Elliott, E. N., 86 n.
Elliott, William Y., 38 n.
Elman, Philip, 79
Emancipation Proclamation, 80
Enforcement Act of 1870, 57
Engle v. Vitale (1962), 89
Essay on Population, 99
Establishment of religion, 24, 35, 36
Everson v. Board of Education, 35

Fair Employment Practices Committee, 1941, 69, 70
Father Divine, 66

Federalist, number *10,* 26, 105; number *51,* 23; number *78,* 98

Fein, L. J., 129 n.

Fifteenth Amendment, 55, 57, 72

Filibuster, 80

First Amendment, *U.S. Constitution,* 24, 31, 35, 36

Fitzhugh, George, 54, 87 n.

Fleming, Billie S., 88 n.

Foner, Philip S., 86 n.

Foreign Conspiracy Against the Liberties of the United States, 30

Fourteenth Amendment, 31, 55, 56, 57, 64, 71, 72, 73, 74, 75, 76, 89, 90, 125

Fox, Guy, 128 n.

Frankfurter, Justice Felix, 32, 33, 34, 90

Freedom Riders, 80

Gallup Poll, 83

Garfinkel, Herbert, 129 n.

Garrison, William Lloyd, 47, 78

Garvey, Marcus, 66

Gee, Wilson, 113, 128 n.

Gomillion v. Lightfoot (1960), 79

Gompers, Samuel, 61

Gillespie, G. T., 50–51, 86 n.

Grant, Madison, 58, 62, 87 n.

Griswold, A. Whitney, 128 n.

Great Case of Liberty of Conscience . . . Briefly Debated and Defended, The, 17

Greene, Evarts B., 39 n.

Grimes, Alan P., 87 n.

Grovey v. Townsend (1935), 71, 72

Handlin, Oscar, 61, 66, 87 n.

Harlan, Justice John M. (Grandfather), 56, 58

Harlan, Justice John M. (Grandson), 91

Harper, William, 52, 53, 86 n., 87 n.

Harrington, Michael, 127 n.

Harris, Louis, 68

Hay, John, 86 n., 88 n.

Hayne, Senator, 103

Hoar, Samuel, 101

Hofstadter, Richard, 128 n.

Holcombe, Arthur N., 110, 128 n.

Howard, Jacob, 56

Huguenots, 5, 23

Hutchinson, Anne, 12, 14

Immigration, and religion, 12, 14, 23, 27–30; and race, 60–63, 66; and urbanization, 111, 112, 115–16

Indians, American, 42–5

Institutes of the Christian Religion, 4

Interstate Commerce Commission, 80

Jackson, Andrew, 104

Jackson, Justice Robert H., 35

Japanese, 60, 63

Javits, Senator Jacob, 78, 81, 88 n.

Jay, John, 112

Jefferson, Thomas, 24, 27, 28, 30, 31, 48, 112, 114

Jenkins, William Sumner, 85 n., 86 n.

Jesuits, 14, 16

Jews, 20, 22, 23, 27, 28, 29, 30, 32

"Jim Crow" laws, 57

Johnson, Richard M., 47

Johnson, Thomas H., 38 n.

Jones, Samuel, 102, 127 n.

Julian, George W., 113

Kennedy, President John F., 68, 82

Kent, James, 101

Key, V. O., Jr., 122, 123, 129 n.

King, Martin Luther, Jr., 80
Knier, Charles M., 128 n.
"Know-Nothings," 29
Kolko, Gabriel, 109, 110, 127 n.
Ku Klux Klan, 66

Lazarus, Emma, 64
Lestchinsky, Jacob, 39 n.
Letter Concerning Toleration of 1689, by John Locke, 9, 11
Letters from an American Farmer, 25
Liberator, 47, 49
Lincoln, Abraham, 48, 85
Lincoln, Thomas, 101
Lipset, Seymour Martin, 88 n.
Locke, John, 24, 38 n., 95, 125, 126 n.
Logan, Rayford W., 55, 87 n.
Luther, Martin, 24
Lutheran, 16, 18

McCarran-Walter Immigration Act of 1952, 64
McDonald, Neil A., 38 n.
McLane, Louis, 48
McLaughlin, Judge, 125
McLaurin v. Oklahoma State Regents (1950), 74
Madison, James, 26, 27, 31, 36, 105
Majority rule, 95, 111, 118, 125, 126
Malthus, Thomas, 99
Marshall, Thurgood, 75
Mathews, Donald R., 88 n.
Mennonites, 18
Miller, Perry, 38 n.
Milton, George Fort, 128 n.
Mims, Edwin, Jr., 127 n.
Missouri Compromise, 49
Missouri ex. rel. Gaines v. Canada (1938), 72
"Mixed government," 99, 101

Moorish-American Science Temple, 66
Morison, Samuel E., 88 n., 127 n.
Morse, Samuel F. B., 29
Myers, Gustavus, 39 n.
Myrdal, Gunnar, 86 n.

Nation, The, 59
National Association for the Advancement of Colored People, 65, 74, 81
National Labor Union, 60
National Origins Act of 1929, 64
National origins system, 62
Nedham, Marchmont, 99
Negroes, colonization of, 46-7; employment, 66, 69, 70, 73; lynching, 65; slavery, 48-50, 52-4; slave trade, 45-6, 60-61; suffrage, 55, 57, 71, 72; *see also*, Segregation
Newsweek poll of July 1963, 68
Newton, Isaac, 24
Nicolay, John G., 86 n., 88 n.
Noah, Rabbi Mordecai, 28
Nordic superiority, 64, 65
Norris, Senator George W., 111
Northwest Ordinance of 1787, 22
Notes on Virginia, 30, 112
Nott, Josiah C., 50, 52
Nye, Russel B., 128 n.

Oregon Bill of Rights, 1857, 55
Our Country, 115

Pan-Africanism, 66
Passing of the Great Race, The, 62
"Peace Movement," 66
Peek, George A., Jr., 127 n.
Penn, William, 15, 17, 25
Place of Agriculture in American Life, The, 113
Plessy v. Ferguson (1896), 57, 58, 67, 71
Prayers in public schools, 30, 34

Presbyterian, 16, 18, 21, 23, 34
President's Committee on Civil Rights of 1946, 69
Protestant churches, 3–6, 15–18, 20, 21, 27–35
Prothro, James W., 88 n.
Puritans, 9, 16, 20

Quakers, 12, 13, 14, 15, 17, 18, 23, 34
Quincy, Josiah, 101
Quota Law of 1921, 111

"Released time" programs, 30, 34–5
Religious freedom, antecedent conditions of, 5
Religious freedom, Jefferson's bill for establishing, 22
Remonstrance Against a Bill Establishing a Provision for Teachers of the Christian Religion in Virginia, 36
Roberts, Justice Owen, 72
Roman Catholic Church, 3–6, 8, 13, 15–18, 20, 21, 23, 25–35
Roosevelt, Franklin D., 54, 68, 69
Rural Versus Urban Political Power, 93
Rutledge, Justice Wiley, 32

Sachar, Howard M., 39 n.
Schlesinger, Joseph A., 129 n.
Segregation, 50, 52–4, 56–8, 69–76, 78, 80, 82
"Segregation and the South," 52
"Separate but equal," 67, 74, 77
Separation of Church and State, 5, 18, 19, 24, 29, 34, 36
Seventeenth Amendment, 96
Seward, George F., 87 n.
Shelley v. Kraemer (1948), 73
Simple Cobbler of Aggawam, The, 14

Sixteenth Amendment, 109
Smith, Henry Nash, 128 n.
Smith, J. Allen, 127 n.
Smith v. Allwright (1944), 72
South Carolina Exposition, 103
"Southern Manifesto," 78
Southern Politics, 122
Stampp, Kenneth M., 85 n.
Standard Metropolitan Statistical Areas, 92
Stanton, William, 86 n.
Stephens, William D., 60, 87
Stokes, Anson Phelps, 38 n., 39 n.
Stouffer, Samuel A., 88 n.
Strong, Josiah, 62, 87 n., 115–17, 128 n.
Student Christian Leadership Conference, 81
Student Nonviolent Coordinating Committee, 81
Sweatt v. Painter (1950), 74
Sweet, William W., 39 n.

Taper, Bernard, 88 n.
Tax support for parochial schools, 30, 35, 36
Thirteenth Amendment, 55, 109
Thirty-Nine Articles of Faith, 4, 7
Thompson, Edgar T., 85 n.
Thorpe, Francis N., 39 n., 87 n.
Tocqueville, Alexis de, 28, 39 n.
Toleration Act of 1689, 18
Toleration, religious, 8–9, 12, 13, 14, 16, 22
Touro Synagogue, 22
Treatise of the Right of Suffrage, 102
Truman, Harry S., 69
Trumbull, Joseph, 100
Turgot, Anne Robert Jacques, 99
Turner, Frederick Jackson, 113, 115
Tuskegee, Alabama, 79

Tussman, Joseph, 87 n., 88 n.
Twentieth Century City, The, 116

U.S. Civil Rights Commission, 81
U.S. Commission on Civil Rights
   Report of 1961, 65, 67
United States v. Reese (1876), 57
Universal Negro Improvement
   Association, 66
Urban League, 65, 81

Virginia Constitution of 1776, Bill
   of Rights, 22

Ward, Nathaniel, 9, 14, 38 n.
Warren, Chief Justice Earl, 76, 77
Washington, Booker T., 65
Washington, Bushrod, 47
Washington, George, 22
Webster, Daniel, 101, 103
White primaries, 71, 72
Williams, Roger, 7, 9–11, 12, 14,
   18, 19, 33, 34, 38 n., 39 n.
Williamson, Chilton, 127 n.
Winslow, Ola Elizabeth, 38 n.

Zorach v. Clauson (1952), 35